Choose to Live
Each Day Fully

Choose to Live Each Day Fully

A 365-Day Guide
to Transforming Your Life
from Ordinary to Extraordinary

Susan Smith Jones, Ph.D.

Celestial Arts
Berkeley, California

The health suggestions and recommendations in this book are based on the training, research, and personal experiences of the author. Because each person and each situation is unique, the author and publisher encourage the reader to check with his or her physician or other health professional before using any procedure outlined in this book. The publisher does not advocate the use of any particular diet or health program, but believes that the information in this book should be available to the public.

Cover design by Ken Scott
Text design and composition by FORM FOLLOWS FUNCTION
First printing, 1994

Library of Congress Cataloging-in-Publication Data

Jones, Susan Smith
    Choose to live each day fully : a 365 day guide to transforming your life from ordinary to extraordinary / Susan Smith Jones.
        p.   cm.
    ISBN 0-89087-713-0
    1. Spiritual life.   2. Devotional calendars.   I. Title.
BL624.J655   1994
291.4'3—dc20   94-332
                                                             CIP

3 4 5 6 7 8 9 10 / 99 98 97

Dedication

This book is lovingly dedicated to my best friend, my Mom, June B. Smith, for her continual support and for being a shining example of unconditional love and forgiveness in my life.

I would also like to dedicate this book to Helen Guppy, Julia Chambers, and Lynn Carroll, my personal angels, who always love me unconditionally and lift me up through the most challenging times of my life.

Acknowledgements

I want to express my gratitude to the following people:

To June B. Smith, my best friend and mother, for teaching me about unconditional love, to believe in myself, and go after my dreams.

To Pamela Davis, for giving me the idea for this book and for always seeing the best in me even when I didn't share the same vision.

To Lynn Carroll, Mary A. Tomlinson, Helen Guppy, Donica and Bev Beath, Kathy Martelli, Gloria Hill, Dianne Warren, Dee Wilkie, Jamie Carr, Letitia Wims, and June Chambers, my special female friends who have blessed and enriched my life with their tenderhearted friendship and loving support.

To David Hinds and Mary Ann Anderson at Celestial Arts, and Sal Glynn, for believing in me and my vision and for their encouraging, gentle, support.

To Paramahansa Yogananda, my spiritual teacher, who, for the last twenty-five years, has taught me that what is most essential is invisible to the eye. It can only be seen and felt with the heart.

To my guardian angels, my constant celestial companions, who guide me every step of the way with their affectionate attention, enlivening my day-to-day activities.

Introduction

Hello,

I am delighted to have this opportunity of being a part of your life for the next year through this book. From more than a decade of traveling internationally to give lectures, workshops, and do consulting, and from the countless letters I receive every year, it's very clear that everyone wants to enrich the quality of his or her life—to make their life extraordinary, a true celebration. There is nothing that you cannot do, be, or have. *Choose to Live Each Day Fully* will show you how.

Each daily lesson is written to inspire you to live more fully which to me means to live healthfully, passionately, joyfully, and peacefully. Think of this book as a confidant, a counselor, a teacher, a diary, a progress report, or a self-improvement manual. Its purpose and uses are really up to you. Read one lesson everyday for the next year, preferably in the morning, as a positive and life-affirming way to start your day. Choose to take a few minutes each day to study the lesson and to find ways you can incorporate the information into your daily life. You may want to spend an extra day or two on some of the lessons or mark the pages you want to return to when the year is up. Remember, "As we think, so we become." Read and repeat the daily affirmations at the bottom of each day's lesson to yourself in the morning, then often throughout the day, to help you absorb its meaning and embrace it in your life.

When you have need of some extra guidance and insight in addition to the daily lesson, take this book and open it randomly and see what blessing serendipity has to offer you for that particular day. Besides using this book on a daily basis, you can also use it whenever the need or desire arises. It is designed to serve your needs. Think of this book as a friend calling on you everyday, or whenever you need some extra support, and empowering you to live more fully.

Since being healthy is a top priority for most people these days, in every other thirty-day period, I focus the lessons on "Be Healthy" so you can make and experience changes in your wellness lifestyle each month. In some of the pages, I recommend products that I personally use; they are really terrific and worth looking into. Every other month, under the heading of "Celebrate Life," I provide everything you need to know to create the life you have imagined—your highest vision for yourself. However you choose to use this book, you will be able to see yourself growing, changing, and becoming more of a master of your life. Knowledge is power and applying that knowledge is empowerment.

As you follow the guidance and integrate the ideas of each lesson into your life, your understanding and receptivity will increase and you'll be able to see yourself more clearly and discover what you need to do to transform your life. Note the patterns of your life, set goals for yourself, and pay attention to how you meet challenges, create solutions, and take responsibility for your life. Unwanted habit patterns or chronic situations that limit your personal growth can readily be changed once you recognize and own them. Choose behavior, belief, or value alternatives that will enhance and enrich your life.

All of us are divine beings in a physical body and we are connected to the loving Source which created us. It makes no difference who or what we are, what training or education we've had, what race we come from, or our age. We've all been given a mission of healing ourselves and learning more about love and our connection to God. Inner peace is the result of self-healing. The inner peace of self-healing can restore our connectedness to God and to all other humans and, in accomplishing this common goal, we will bring world peace into reality. We are all responsible for working very hard on ourselves and sharing our discoveries of our personal healing paths with others.

If this book moves you into action and enriches your life, do yourself and others a favor by giving copies as gifts. Remember, we're here to see each other through on our journeys.

Don't let your commitment to live fully and celebrate life take a back seat to anything. You wake up into a whole new world every morning. Today is brand new. Today can be a new beginning where you can start fresh and you can choose to make this next year the best and most rewarding of your life. You have a choice. *You always have a choice.* And you don't have to be the same person today that you were yesterday. You can choose your direction and your response every conscious moment of your life.

It's all up to you. I salute your great adventure and commitment to choose to live each day fully.

Peace be with you,

Susan S. Jones

Resources begin on page 367.

Index to Days begins on page 375.

The Art of Living Fully

To live fully means living passionately, peacefully, joyfully, and healthfully while celebrating and playing at this game of life. In order to do this, look at your life from a higher perspective rather than getting caught up in the day-to-day inconsequential matters. Love all aspects of your life. Be grateful for your challenges for they make you grow and become stronger.

Living fully means playing at work and working at your play. Nurture your spiritual life and bring your spirituality into every part of your life. Make everything you do sacred for every step you take is on holy ground. Play at this game of life and live in alignment with your integrity and highest vision. Commit to becoming master of your life and captain of your soul.

*This is my life and starting today, I commit
to living passionately and fully, letting the loving
Source that created me enrich my life everyday.*

Heart-to-Heart

In your relationships with others, what really matters is the heart-to-heart or love connection. Educational background, occupation, skin color, shape, size, age ... none of that matters. That's just gift wrapping—a special covering unique to everyone—and your essence is a spiritual being. At the level of the heart, all people are connected by love.

Find ways to let others know you appreciate them. When you continually find fault and criticize another, they wither up like a flower without water. Show love and appreciation and they will blossom. Isn't that what you want—to be loved, respected, and appreciated? It's so simple.

Today find ways to love and appreciate others.

*I choose to see the positive side of everyone
and love and appreciate the people in my life.*

Intuition

Right this moment you have a voice within you available to give you guidance in any area of your life. How tuned in are you to this voice within? When you get a message, do you usually write it off as nothing? The more you pay attention to your intuition, the more you'll find yourself in the right place at the right time.

So how can you develop the intuitive side of your being? The best way is just to sit still and listen. Turn within and pay attention. Take some time to be still, turn within, and listen to your inner voice guiding you every step of the way.

Two marvelous books I recommend to support you in nurturing your intuition are *Practical Intuition* by Laura Day and *Anatomy of the Spirit* by Caroline Myss, Ph.D.

In trust and gratitude, I take time each day
to turn within to the ever-present guidance.

Lighten Up

Don't take yourself and your life so seriously and forget that life was meant to be a great adventure to be lived fully. When you become too serious, life looses its luster and you have a hard time being happy.

Choose to look at problems that arise in your life as opportunities to grow, change, learn more about yourself, and live more fully. Keep in mind this old Scottish saying as you venture through your day: "Angels fly because they take themselves lightly."

I embrace each day with enthusiasm and a joy of life.
I laugh my way to enlightenment.

Being Childlike

Young children are the greatest teachers of how to live a great adventure and how to choose an attitude of positive thinking. Have you ever seen children water the plants, or help with the dishes, or vacuum? They can't wait to participate. They act as though it's just about the most exciting thing they've ever done. What a wonderful quality that is, to be excited about every part of life.

Go through your day today and look at everything and everyone as though it's for the first time. Look with fresh eyes and an open heart.

I choose to see everything in my life today
as though it was for the first time,
and let my inner child come out and play.

Participate in Life

Start participating in life's adventures rather than saying, "One day I'll do that, or I'll go there." Take a moment to write a list of all the things you'd like to do but haven't — maybe because you thought you'd look silly, or that you might fail, or because you are afraid.

Would you like to learn to ski, climb Mt. Whitney, bake bread, play the piano, parasail, or ride a horse? Which of these things that you've listed can you do right away? Do it today or this week. Don't wait until it's too late. This is an essential part of making your life a grand celebration.

*I seek out new adventures in my life
and rise above all fear and hesitation.*

Emotions and Health

When feelings are denied or repressed, lethargy, boredom, and a sense of deadness or numbness toward life may be the unfortunate consequences. Those who are unaccustomed to dealing with feelings in healthy ways often seek out other means to cover them up or distract themselves.

Make friends with your emotional, feeling self. Accept strong emotions as valuable feedback telling you that something is in need of attention. Write an angry letter and then tear it up; be out in Nature and pay attention to her guidance; pay attention to the whisperings of your heart; talk about your feelings to someone you trust and with whom you feel safe.

It's okay to be afraid. Feel the fear and move through it. Don't try to chase these emotions away or deny your feelings. Look at them, express and own them, then move on.

I embrace my emotions without fear.

Expectancy

Expect only the best in your life. If you see your world according to what surrounds you right now, you're judging by appearances and limiting what you're going to have.

Trust in the universe and the power within you, regardless of appearances. As you change your consciousness, your beliefs, and thoughts about yourself, you change your life. Because thought creates form, the very thing you believe becomes reality. Choose not to get discouraged or upset when things don't seem to go as you had hoped they would. With every adversity comes the seed for wonderful growth, change, and opportunity.

*I place all my cares and worries in the Spirit
and trust that everything is now unfolding
for my highest good.*

Seeing with Your Heart

What is truly essential is invisible to the eye and can only be seen with the heart. See more with your heart and your life will become a wonderful adventure.

Let this day be one in which you see beyond the appearances of people, places, and things and look with your heart to what's important.

I look beyond appearances to the love of God
all around me as well as within me.

Sense of Humor

When was the last time you really laughed? Laughter is the lubricant of life. It's the elixir that enables you to experience the fullness and joy of life. Being able to laugh at yourself and the incongruities of everyday situations is the best way to quell stress and to enjoy life.

Before the day is over, find at least three things you can really laugh about. You might have to look hard but it's all in your attitude about life. Laugh and your life will brighten up.

*I put on a happy face and radiate health
and happiness in everything I do.*

Commitment

A commitment is the honoring of a decision. Make your word count. How do you expect someone to make a commitment to you or expect you'll follow through on a commitment to them unless you first are committed to yourself?

If you are ready for commitment, you will immediately arrange your personal circumstances so that your lifestyle totally supports your commitment. You will do whatever it takes, whatever you need to do to order your life, and consciously focus on what is important.

By really committing to yourself, by following through on your convictions and decisions and allowing nothing to stand in the way of your becoming master of your life, you will gain tremendous power.

All things are working together for good in my life.

Seize the Day

Today is a new beginning. No longer do you need to repeat the past or worry about the uncertain future. Live your life the best you can today and the future will take care of itself.

The world is here to give you what you want. It is always saying "yes" to you. The course of your life does not have to be confined to the restrictions of the past.

Embrace this new day and feel recharged by the thought of starting fresh. Be enthusiastic about the possibilities before you. Let go of everything that is not for your highest good. Release your bad habits. Start taking better care of yourself. Begin with the little things and the big things will take care of themselves.

I use my creative power to bring the best to me. My highest vision is waiting for me to claim it now.

Stress and Breathing

Stress is an inevitable fact of life but you don't have to choose to let it get the best of you. The more stressed you feel, the more shallow your breathing becomes. Breathing consciously can relieve tension, help quiet fear, and relieve pain. So before you reach for the aspirins or antacid tablets, do some deep breathing. Make periods of deep breathing a regular part of each day.

I love and accept myself just the way I am.
I take good care of myself.

Spend Your Time Wisely

Spend your time wisely and don't waste it with negative thinking. Think of your time like money. Recognize that you have only a certain amount on hand. Use it to do what is important to you.

Take time to turn within and discover what's really important to you. Think of dreams that you have had for a long time, then go for what really matters to you. The time is now. Isn't it better not to wait?

Focusing on the present heals my fear of the unknown.

Enjoy the Simple Things

Don't wait until it's too late to enjoy the simple pleasures of life. What can you enjoy right now? How about the change of seasons or how beautiful the moon and stars look in the night sky? Or the family and friends who so wonderfully enrich your life?

Look around you today and pay attention to the many simple pleasures in your life.

Every moment in my life is love-focused.

An Indian Prayer

See the One in everything. The following is a Sioux Indian prayer.

O Great Spirit,
Whose voice I hear in the winds,
And whose breath gives life to all the world,
hear me. I am small and weak. I need your
strength and wisdom.

Let me walk in beauty, and make my eyes
ever behold the red and purple sunset.

Make my hands respect the things you have
made and my ears sharp to hear your voice.

Make me wise so that I may understand the
things you have taught my people.

Let me learn the lessons you have hidden
in every leaf and rock.

I seek strength, not to be greater than my
brother, but to fight my greatest
enemy—myself.

Make me always ready to come to you with
clean hands and straight eyes.

So when life fades, as the fading sunset,
my spirit may come to you without shame.

I walk in love with God as my source.

Affirmation Treatment

Practice love and forgiveness towards yourself and everyone with this reminder from Unity minister John Strickland.

I love you; I bless you; I appreciate you; I forgive you; and I release you to your highest good.

I am love; I am blessed; I am appreciated; I am forgiven; and I am released to my highest good.

You love yourself; you bless yourself; you appreciate yourself; you forgive yourself; and you release yourself to your highest good.

I love myself; I bless myself; I appreciate myself; I forgive myself; and I release myself to my highest good.

As I forgive, so I am forgiven.

Unconditional Love

Mother Teresa is one of the world's best examples of someone who loves unconditionally. She lives with love in her heart and does everything within her power to reduce human sorrow. She has lived among the world's most impoverished people, trying to ease their misery and save them from starvation.

By her shining example, Mother Teresa has proven that love is the strongest force on earth. With love, there is always a way.

When I follow the path of love,
the universe supports me.

Tips for Staying in Love

Dr. Barbara De Angelis, internationally recognized as an expert on relationships and personal growth and author of several books including *Secrets About Men Every Woman Should Know,* offers the following advice on how to stay in love.

1. Work on your relationship—don't wait until the relationship stops working to start working on it.

2. Always communicate the complete truth—holding back makes it impossible for love to keep flowing.

3. Never miss an opportunity to say "I love you." Telling your partner "I love you" doesn't merely convey information, it creates a channel for love to flow.

4. Decide you would rather love than be *right*—make up quickly after a fight.

5. Never try to pretend that things are fine when they're not. Holding negative emotions will only build up resentment towards your partner and you'll end up turning off.

I attract positive, supportive friends and lovers.

Surrounding Ourselves with Life

If we live in an environment of living things, we feel better. We have more vitality, more energy, a healthier immune system, and have a more positive attitude about life. Some living things that can enhance our lives include plants, flowers, and animals such as dogs, cats, birds, and even little pigs.

Dogs can have a salutary effect on our well-being. A veterinary researcher in England says dogs can be an invaluable early warning system for people prone to epileptic seizures, diabetic coma, and possibly even heart attacks. In his latest study, Andrew Edney, D.V.M. looked at 121 dogs who had reportedly given warning of an impending seizure. Among the telltale behaviors—as much as forty-five minutes before the episode—were barking, jumping up and nuzzling, trying to get the victim to lie down, herding him or her to safety, or alerting others in the household. Other studies suggest that some dogs may alert diabetic owners to impending hypoglycemic comas, and Edney theorizes that someday dogs may be trained to help heart attack victims recognize danger signals.

What can you do today to bring some living things into your life? One of the easiest ways is to get a plant or some fresh flowers.

I feel a special connection with all life
and I choose to surround myself with living things.

Basics of Meditation

Meditation breaks through the everyday world of thoughts and tension to create greater inner peace, insight, and enlightenment. The basis of meditation is to focus on an object, a visualization, or a breath, and to keep your awareness on that point. By this process of focusing on one point, the internal noise is lessened, your mind is quieter, and your energy level is higher.

There are many ways to meditate. Some meditations use sound, or mantras, as a focus. A common mantra is OM, pronounced with a long oooh and a short mm sound. You can also meditate by watching your breath: concentrate on the inhale and exhale, and keep your eyes relaxed and open by gazing at a point on the floor or wall a few feet away from you. Meditations on the third eye, the point between the eyes and about an inch above them in the middle of the forehead, or the crown chakra at the top of the head can be used for internally focused meditations. Use different methods to find the technique that gives you the best results.

To improve meditation, find a fairly comfortable position to sit in. Sit with your back and neck straight; this will make the energy flow more easily through your spine. Be awake and alert; the higher your energy, the easier it will be to focus. It's best to meditate on an empty stomach.

When I look to my Source,
I am guided to make choices for my highest good.

Protecting Your Privacy

Just because your home telephone is ringing or there is a knock at your door doesn't mean you have to stop what you're doing to answer it. If you're too busy with other things or simply don't feel like talking, let it ring. The world won't come to an end. If the call is really important, the other person will try you again.

When my telephone rings, I can decide to answer it or not. My privacy is very important to me.

Practice Caring Behavior

It takes so little to do so much. Write a list of specific little things that your partner could do to make you feel more content. Have him or her write a list, too. Examples: Give me a bath and wash my hair; initiate sex; hold my hand in the movies; open the door for me; take me out to dinner so I won't have to spend time in the kitchen. Exchange lists. For a week, try to do three things on your partner's list every day. At the end of each day, acknowledge what your partner did and point out what you did that he or she did not notice.

I always find ways to do special things for my partner.
I know that in giving we truly receive.

The Gift of a Letter

Letter writing seems to be a lost art, especially in this computerized, fast-paced age. Letters can be magical; they document the chapters in our lives and provide an uninhibited view of everyday life. They capture moments in your life and linger on when the letter is read and reread—much different than a telephone call.

A letter is a gift which gives you time to think and ponder what's been written. A letter doesn't require immediate attention and can be saved until you have time to sit down and relax and savor every word. For some inspiring reading, try *The Gift of a Letter* by Alexandra Stoddard. Whose day could you brighten by writing a letter?

Today I choose to write a letter
and let someone special know that I care.

The Forty-Day Prosperity Plan

One of the best books on prosperity and creating what you want is *The Abundance Book* by John Randolph Price. Following his forty-day program will make a profound difference in your level of prosperity.

Establish a specific date to start your program, writing down your statement, and say the affirmations he provides. Here are some of his affirmations.

God is lavish, unfailing Abundance, the rich omnipresent substance of the Universe. This all providing Source of infinite prosperity is individualized as me—the Reality of me.

I lift up my mind and heart to be aware, to understand, and to know that the Divine Presence I AM is the Source and Substance of all my good.

I believe in God as the source of my infinite supply which manifests through my life as abundance and prosperity on all levels.

Spending Time Alone

Spending time alone, in the peace of your own company, you realize that you are never alone. Without that time of solitude, you won't be your best for others. It's essential for living fully and celebrating life. Where in your life can you set aside daily time for yourself, even if it's only for a few minutes?

Henry David Thoreau wrote in his inspiring book *Walden,* "I find it wholesome to be alone the greater part of the time. To be in company, even with the best, is soon wearisome and dissipating. I love to be alone. I never found the companion that was so companionable as solitude. We are for the most part more lonely when we go abroad among men than when we stay in our chambers."

I love to spend time alone; I can be true to myself and hear the whisperings of God.

Sincerity

Henry David Thoreau believed every person should perform his own duty with sincerity. "Be resolutely and faithfully what you are," he wrote in his journal; "be humbly what you aspire to be. Be sure you give men the best of your wares, though they be poor enough, and the gods will help you lay up a better store for the future. Man's noblest gift to man is his sincerity, for it embraces his integrity also...."

I am sincere in my relations with others because I live in the knowledge that God is my source and all my needs are constantly met.

Not Judging by Appearances

When you judge your life by appearances, you are going to limit what you'll have. Trust in the universe, the power within, and always put your focus (your visions, thoughts, affirmations) on what you want. Your future does not have to be a duplication of the past.

No matter what's happening in your life right now, continue to focus on your goals, on the abundance you desire and deserve, on the job you want, and on the relationship you want. This idea of staying focused is one of the most important things you can do to change your life for the better. By switching your thinking to your goals, you'll begin to move closer to them and they will begin to move toward you. Remarkable things happen when you live with a positive expectancy.

Thought times feeling equals manifestation.

Living my highest potential is just a thought away.
I desire and deserve the best that life has to offer.

Follow Your Heart

As a beloved First Lady, Eleanor Roosevelt was an indefatigable champion for overcoming personal struggles and living a fulfilling life. She has much to teach about the importance of acting upon your convictions and ignoring your critics. She was never afraid to stand up for what she believed in. It was Eleanor who said that no one can make you feel inferior without your consent. Over the years, she lent emotional and financial support to a number of unpopular causes, including housing for the poor, relief for Jewish refugees, and civil rights for African Americans.

Because of her position, Eleanor was a favorite target for critics, yet she never wavered in her commitment to what she believed to be right. "Every woman in public life," she once explained, "needs to develop skin as tough as rhinoceros hide." Only one thing about these attacks bothered her, their effect on her friends and family. In 1940, she wrote to a friend, "I am sorry these attacks are causing my friends so much anguish, but I intend to keep on saying what has to be said." This rare combination of courage, grit, and compassion is Eleanor Roosevelt's greatest legacy.

*I am worthy to receive
the unlimited offerings of the universe.*

Let Your Dreams Take Flight

It's important to have goals in your life. You can define and shape your goals through visualization and by writing them down on paper. What do you want in life? Today think about and write down your goals in all these areas: relationships, career, health, lifestyle, and spirituality. For example, for health you might write, "My goal for health: my body is fit and trim and I am experiencing radiant health. I have lots of energy and a zest for life."

Set a time schedule for this goal to be achieved. You might make monthly, quarterly, bi-annually, and yearly goals. When you achieve them, rewrite them.

Visualizing your goals on a daily basis instills them with power. The most powerful weapon you have is your imagination. Let your dreams take flight.

I am excited and passionate about life.

Cutting Down on Fat

If you want radiant health and to be free from disease, cut down your fat intake. More and more evidence is leading to a ten percent fat diet for optimum health. Did you know that it's easier to eat a lot less fat than it is to cut back only a little? After five to six weeks on a ten percent fat diet, your taste buds will begin to change. Fatty foods you once enjoyed will begin to taste too greasy while foods that once seemed impossibly bland will become tastier. Not only that, because you'll be eating so little fat, you'll easily lose excess weight while never feeling hungry or deprived.

Here's how to tell how much fat you're getting. First you'll need to keep a food diary. Jot down the calorie and fat content of each food you eat. At the end of each day, calculate the all-important fat percentage. Multiply your total daily intake of fat (in grams) by nine (the number of calories in each fat gram), then divide this number by your total daily calories. If this number is above ten percent, you must find ways to cut out more fat. After several weeks, you'll be able to judge your fat intake without using the diary. A great, practical book is *Get the Fat Out: 501 Simple Ways to Cut the Fat in Any Diet* by Victoria Moran.

My body radiates health and vitality because I choose foods that are low in fat and high in nutritional value.

Tune into Your Body

If you listen to your body, you will discover that it actually talks to you. When you get a headache, your body is trying to tell you something. Listen to your body's signals and communication with health and peace as your goals. The key is your willingness to listen and act.

If you feel a pain, your body is trying to tell you something. Maybe you need to eat better or exercise regularly. Or maybe you need to get more sleep and live a more balanced life.

The human body is beautifully robust and efficiently and effectively equipped to meet your problems. It's normal to be healthy and it's your divine birthright to be well. Listen to your body. Respect and appreciate it. Take loving care of it.

This body in which I live is my home
and I lovingly care for it.

KYO-GREEN

Chlorophyll is very beneficial for the body and has been used for years to successfully treat oral diseases, chronic ulcers, kidney stones, acute infections of the upper respiratory tract and sinuses, and for overall body cleansing and rejuvenation.

Nutritionists believe that the best sources of chlorophyll are wheat and barley grasses, kelp, alfalfa, and an algae called chlorella.

Just two tablespoons of barley grass has as much beta-carotene as a serving of spinach. Rich in vitamin A and beta-carotene, wheat and barley grass lead to the formation and maintenance of healthy skin, bones, teeth, and mucous membranes and play a role in healthy human reproduction. These grasses are also a rich source of vitamin B_1 and B_2 which means they help maintain a strong nervous system.

Kelp is a rich source of vitamin C and a number of important minerals, especially calcium, potassium, magnesium, and iodine. Research has found that it boosts the body's own immune system, allowing it to combat cancer.

All of these are found in *KYO-GREEN* (see *Resources*). Both the plants and juices are used in a special drying process that protects nutrients and retains dietary fiber. The fine powder easily dissolves in water and fruit and vegetable juice.

*Nature has provided all the nutrients
I need to be radiantly healthy.*

Building Stronger Ankles

For years coaches and athletes have considered the quadriceps, located on the anterior thigh, as being the important muscle used in running. The thigh muscles actually do less for runners than at first thought; their main function is to support the body when the foot makes contact with the ground.

Strong ankles are the support pillars for squats, deadlifts, calf raises, and many other exercises. You're only as strong as your weakest link, so strengthen those ankles!

The force generated to propel the body forward originates in the hip and ankle joints. In fact, the ankle joint can contribute up to sixty percent of the total force involved in propelling a runner forward. The hip joint, in both flexion (bringing the thigh forward) and in extension (bringing the thigh backward), contributes anywhere from thirty to fifty percent of the total force generated.

Strengthening these joint areas is essential in improving running performance, jogging, and brisk walking. Running or jogging figure eights will help strengthen your ankles. So will walking barefoot in the sand and pressing your foot both inwardly and outwardly against the sand. You can also do the same foot presses against a wall.

I walk with a bounce in my step
and a smile on my face.

Psychoneuroimmunology

There's an exciting, new field of science called psychoneuroimmunology, or PNI, which deals with how your mind can effect your immune system's incredibly complex network of organs, vessels, and white blood cells. Research in this field indicates that the immune system, brain, and other vital body systems such as the endocrine system, communicate/connect with and influence one another.

Your body can cope with disease and heal itself if you are not under lots of stress. Well-managed stress helps to keep your immune system healthy.

While you can't totally avoid the pressure in this world and it's often difficult to live without stress, you can seek out balance and choose to live more simply.

De-stressors: 1. Exercise.
                 2. Meditate.
                 3. Let go and let God.

I can manage the stress in my life
and encourage my health every day.

Common Sense and Radiant Health

The secret to living a life full of aliveness and radiant health comes from using common sense, living simply, and working close to nature. Nature has provided everything you need to live your highest potential.

Eat moderately. Eat when hungry, not just because the clock dictates it's mealtime. Select a variety of fresh foods every day. Your foods should be natural, whole, and pure. At least half of your diet should be based on raw foods meaning plenty of fresh fruits and vegetables. Stay away from too many dairy and animal products. Avoid foods made with white sugar, white flour, preservatives, additives, and other processing elements. Drink plenty of pure water. And be grateful for and bless the foods you eat. Think of your body as God's precious temple and make healthy choices that support your highest well-being.

Being healthy is a top priority.
I am committed to living my highest potential.

Foods that Promote Health

Green Magma is a powdered juice made from barley grass that offers nature's own perfect balance of vitamins and minerals. Young barley grass grown in some of the world's most fertile soil near the Pacific Ocean is harvested, then transported to a state-of-the-processing facility just minutes away. Barley grass is flowing with beta-carotene, live enzymes such as superoxide dismutase (or SOD), vitamins C, E, B_1, B_2, B_3, and B_6 (B vitamins are catalysts essential for converting food into energy), amino acids, and much more. Powdered brown rice, grown without pesticides or chemical fertilizers, is mixed with the concentrated juice. The rice increases the levels of B vitamins and helps the fine powder bind together after it is spray-dried at low temperatures.

People who drink Green Magma frequently say they notice a boost in their energy, especially in the afternoons when they need it most. I agree. That's probably because of the supplement's active live enzymes which are essential for proper digestion and assimilation of the valuable vitamins and trace minerals in the foods we consume. Green Magma is available in health food stores and nutrition centers. Look for it, along with Green Essence, Green Magma Senior Formula, and Green Magma Women's Formula-all excellent supplements. For more information, see *Resources*.

Thank you God for your gift of green foods.

Weight Loss Tips

Is it possible to eat more complex carbohydrates and lose weight? You bet it is! Potatoes, squash, and whole grains such as brown rice and bread, if not overeaten, provide your body with energy. Consider this: one gram of carbohydrate has only four calories. A gram of fat has nine calories. Fat gets stored in the body more quickly than carbohydrates. High carbohydrate foods are more bulky than high fat foods and are more satisfying.

Thirty-two cups of air-popped corn has the same number of calories as one cup of dry roasted peanuts. It takes a walk the length of a football field to burn off the calories in one M & M. To walk off the calories of a fast food hamburger, fries, and a malt, you would have to walk the length of 240 football fields. Is it really worth it?

So if you want to lose weight, a diet low in fat and high in complex carbohydrates could be right for you. Take in fewer calories than you burn, of course, and consider some low-impact aerobics like brisk walking, cycling, and stair climbing. Exercise combined with a low fat, high nutrient diet is an unbeatable combination if you want to lose weight. A fantastic book to read is *Discovery: The Common Sense Weight Solution* by Jacklyn Kay Brown. Adopt a healthy lifestyle and commit to it.

My body is fit and trim and beautifully shaped, easily and effortlessly.

Drink Plenty of Pure Water

Your body is made up of sixty to seventy-five percent water and daily replenishment is essential for optimum health. In your lifetime, you are going to drink 58,333 pounds of water. That comes to 7,000 gallons.

Make sure the water you drink is pure. You may want to consider getting either bottled water or filter it at the tap in your home or office. Use bottled spring or reverse osmosis water if you can.

Drink at least six large glasses, and even twice that much, each day depending on your size, level of activity, time of year, and thirst. Avoid drinking with your meals as that dilutes digestive enzymes and decreases the efficiency of your digestive system.

Each morning have a large glass of warm to hot water with the juice of one quarter fresh lemon. This gets the system moving, helps to prevent constipation, and is wonderful for your skin.

I cleanse and rejuvenate my body
with several glasses of water each day.

Seven-Day Rejuvenation Program

At least four times a year, with the change of each season, follow a rejuvenation program to help detoxify your body and rejuvenate your cells and system.

For seven days, breakfast consists of fresh fruit in season. Between breakfast and lunch, any other kind of fruit or fresh fruit/vegetable juice may be taken. For lunch, have a big, beautiful salad with lots of fresh vegetables, sprouts, leafy greens, and sprinkle a few raw almonds or some raw sunflower seeds on your salad for some quality protein. For a mid-afternoon snack, have a glass of fresh fruit or vegetable juice (made fresh from a juicer) and some raw vegetables, or another piece of fresh fruit. For dinner, have two or three steamed vegetables along with either a grain (such as brown rice) or starch (potatoes, yams, squash). This eating program is light, filling, and rejuvenating because it's high in nutrients and fiber and low in fat.

During this week make sure to get plenty of aerobic exercise and take at least three ten-minute periods every day to do some deep breathing and relaxation exercises. You can also take a few minutes each day to visualize the goals in your life as already accomplished.

What you'll discover with this type of program is you'll feel so good after the seven days you will probably want to continue with many of these practices. For a more detailed rejuvenation program, refer to my book, *Choose to Be Healthy.*

My food choices reflect my love for myself and life.

Power C

Vitamin C maintains homeostasis, the term biologists use to describe staying on an "even keel" when faced with stress, infections, heart disease, cancer, and other conditions. Vitamin C is essential for a smooth-running immune system, and is also an antioxidant.

New methods of preparing this vitamin have added to its effectiveness and tamed it for those who have been put off by its acidity. This new family of mineral ascorbates is called Ester-C Vitamin C, made by the Inter-Cal Corporation (see *Resources*). Ester-C can be found in hundreds of products sold by dozens of distributors. It's non-acidic, so the harshness that might upset your stomach is gone. The unique manufacturing process creates a patented vitamin C complex consisting of ascorbate and C metabolites which enhance cellular absorption and utilization of the ascorbate in Ester-C supplements.

I desire and deserve to be healthy and peaceful.

Breathing Deeply

If you want to be radiantly healthy, make breathing deeply a part of your life.

Diaphragmatic or deep abdominal breathing promotes a more relaxed state. When you inhale deeply, the air goes to the lower part of the lungs. Since gravity pulls more blood into that area, the most efficient passage of oxygen into the blood occurs there, slowing the breath as the body gets more oxygen. It's important to note how closely respiration and the heart are tied. As the breath slows to six to eight breaths per minute and deepens, the heart's job is considerably easier. This could result in a reduction of up to fifty percent in the workload on the cardiovascular system. Also, diaphragmatic breathing has the added bonus of relaxing the muscles of the ribs, chest, and stomach.

So take some time out today and concentrate on your breathing. Breathe in slowly and deeply and then slowly exhale. You'll quickly discover how relaxed and healthy it makes you feel.

With each breath I take, I feel more at peace.
I celebrate life today.

Building Strong Bones

Daily weight-bearing activity is essential to the health of the skeleton. Weight-bearing stress is likely to be the most important factor affecting bone development. The muscles transmit mechanical and bioelectrical signals to the bone, causing it to thicken in response to use.

Your body is meant to be used. Movement of the arms and legs is not enough. What is needed is regular use of the muscles lifting the body's weight against the pull of gravity. Excellent exercise include climbing stairs or stepping up and down on a low step repeatedly, and the best is weight training. Weight training and lifting with all extremities builds stronger, thicker bones in the body.

The 206 bones in my miraculous body
are strong and healthy.

Let There Be Rest

The actual building and strengthening and ren-ovating of the body takes place during rest and sleep, when growth and nutritional processes are at their maximum. Get plenty of sleep every night and don't hes-itate to take a midday nap when circumstances permit.

The way to determine whether you are getting enough rest and sleep in your life is to examine how you feel first thing in the morning. Do you wake up sponta-neously feeling refreshed, without having to rely on an alarm clock? Do you feel prepared for physical and men-tal activity without resorting to coffee or other stimu-lants? Do you wake up with a positive mental attitude? If your answer to any of these questions is no, then you are probably not getting enough sleep. Go to bed ear-lier each night and sleep in on the weekend.

I rest in the peace of God.

Dry Brushing

Dry brushing the body with a natural bristle brush or loofah mitt each day before bathing can be very beneficial. Not only does dry brushing improve the appearance of your skin giving you a healthy glow, but it also helps your body eliminate toxins. Your skin is your largest eliminative organ and dry brushing assists in sloughing off the dead skin cells which lie on the skin's surface. Dry brushing greatly assists in the task of detoxification.

Look for a dry brush at your local health food store. Make sure it has natural bristles (as opposed to nylon or other synthetics) and a long handle so you can reach all those hard-to-get places on your body. You want to start off very gently for the first couple weeks until your skin get used to it.

Brush in circular motions, always moving toward the heart. If there are patches of eczema, skin eruptions, or any other skin condition, avoid brushing the affected areas. Also, avoid brushing the face. This process of dry brushing (do it before you shower or bathe) can be done daily and you'll see and feel a difference before the first week is up.

Every day I am getting younger and more radiant.

In Support of Walking

Women should walk, even if it's not fast enough to be aerobic according to researchers at the Cooper Institute for Aerobics Research in Dallas, Texas. They conducted a study in which 102 sedentary women aged twenty to forty were divided into three walking groups and one control group. Five days a week, all the walkers walked three miles on the track. The aerobic walkers finished in 36 minutes (moving at 5 mph), the brisk walkers finished in 46 minutes (moving at 4 mph), and the strollers finished in 60 minutes (moving at 3 mph).

After 42 weeks, the aerobic walkers were in the best shape (as measured by oxygen capacity). However, HDL ("good") cholesterol levels in the brisk walkers and the strollers rose as much as in the aerobic walkers, and all three groups lost the same amount of weight.

If you are interested in losing some weight, get out and walk six days a week for at least 30 minutes. Combine this with a low fat, high complex carbohydrate diet.

I walk my way to health and vitality.
I love to exercise and do so regularly.

The Power of Juicing

Eating more fresh fruits and vegetables will not only make you healthier but also help to prevent a variety of diseases including heart disease, cancer, and obesity. Fresh juice is a quick, delicious way to consume nutritious fruits and vegetables raw in quantity.

The food you put in your system determines the health of every cell and organ in your body. To experience radiant health and to live fully, you need an abundance of "live" foods. This means uncooked foods such as fruits and vegetables. Other foods, such as nuts, grains, seeds, and legumes, are also live foods.

When you eat fresh fruits and vegetables, your body extracts as liquid what it needs from the fiber, which passes on to the lower digestive tract. When you drink freshly made juice, you are eliminating the digestive process (extracting the liquid from the fiber) and efficiently supplying the body with nutrients. Fresh juice that you make at home in your juicer is much better for you than bottled, canned, or concentrated juices sold in the supermarket. The Juiceman Juicer (see *Resources*) is one of the best home juicers. Fresh juice rejuvenates your body and boosts your immune system so that your body can heal itself.

I support my body temple in rejuvenating itself
by eating a variety of fruits and vegetables,
and drinking fresh juices.

What about
Nutritional Supplements?

Fifty years ago it may have been possible to be radiantly and vibrantly healthy simply by eating wholesome foods and living a wellness lifestyle. But today, very few live a totally balanced, wholesome life-style—eating home grown vital foods, breathing clean air, drinking fresh noncontaminated water, exercising regularly and living stress-free. Living a high-demand, fast-paced, stressful lifestyle places extra requirements upon your body, and you need the additional support and protection that supplements can give. Even if you eat the healthy, plant-based diet recommended in this book, you can't be sure your diet is as nourishing as it should be due to the depletion of soil minerals. And more stress is placed on your body due to chemical and pesticide exposure.

If you smoke, drink alcohol, or take any kind of medi-cation, you need the extra protection that good supple-ments can give you. Even when you exercise, your body creates deleterious free radicals which can be neutral-ized by antioxidants. With all the changes and stresses in your life, you need all the help you can get and nutri-tional support is an important ally.

I provide my body everything it needs
to be radiantly healthy and vitally alive.

Your Lymphatic System

The functions of your lymphatic system are just as important as the beating of your heart. The blood circulatory system transports nutrients to the cells, whereas the lymph carries excess water away from the cells. The lymph system transports important proteins, fats, and hormones to the cells and carries nutrients to the cells that the blood cannot reach. It also maintains your immune system and carries away waste in the body.

Here are some ways to keep your lymph system healthy. Exercise regularly. Your lungs play an important role in helping the lymph to circulate. Breathe deeply several times each day as this also promotes better lymphatic circulation. Give your skin a good dry brushing daily. This helps to open up clogged pores, stimulates blood circulation, and helps tremendously in the movement of lymphatic fluids. Massage is also beneficial for keeping the lymph system healthy. Choose to eat foods as close to the way nature made them as possible and place emphasis on raw foods. Fresh raw fruits and vegetables cleanse the body as well as providing an abundance of nutrients. Make sure you get plenty of pure water everyday as this also helps the lymph system to work efficiently.

*I support my body's natural cleansing system
with fresh food and exercise.*

Cycling

Here are guidelines to help you get the most out of your bike rides:

Ride in low gears. To go faster longer, use a gear low enough to turn the pedals at least seventy times per minute.

Connect to your pedals. Bike pedals with straps to hold your feet allow you to pull up on the pedal while pushing down on the other. This added force can increase your speed by one to two miles per hour. Also, get proper still-soled biking shoes, which allow you to apply more pressure to the pedals.

Lighten up. The lighter your wheels, the easier it will be to get them moving. Sometimes the change can be as easy as having your bike shop switch you to lighter spokes, but it may also be necessary to use a lighter rim or hub.

Top quality. Buy the best quality bike you can afford. Klein Company (see *Resources*) makes excellent road, mountain, and hybrid bikes.

*Exercise is a top priority in my life
and I find ways to be active several times each week.*

Bio-Strath

We want to live longer, glow with vibrant health, reverse the aging process and build up our resistance to disease. To this list, most people would also include desiring more energy, mental clarity, and increased performance. But is there one specific nutritional supplement that will help us achieve all this? Perhaps there is. It's called *Bio-Strath* and it's an excellent herbal food supplement in liquid and tablet form.

A result of accurate, scientifically-based work and based on plasmolysed yeast and wild herbs, *Bio-Strath* has been available for decades in over forty countries around the world. I've included *Bio-Strath* in my health program for over a decade and highly recommend it. It has been found to combat fatigue, lethargy, and nervousness, increase physical and mental efficiency, improve concentration, reinforce the immune defense system and restore vitality. I also like the fact that it is 100 percent natural, virtually manufactured by nature without chemicals, synthetic vitamins or heat. The *Bio-Strath* herbal yeast contains a great variety of vital substances as amino acids, nucleic acids RNA and DNA, vitamins from the B-complex and various minerals and trace elements. Available in health food stores, Bio-Strath also comes in yeast-free drops. For more information, see *Resources.*

I am always seeking ways I can learn more
about being healthy and living to my highest potential.

Getting Trim for Life

If you want to lose weight and keep it off, pay attention to the following.

Visualize yourself fit and trim. Spend at least ten minutes daily visualizing.

Take responsibility. You can make yourself fit and trim.

Seek out help if you have a hard time staying motivated on your own.

Go slowly. Plan so that you deliberately lose your weight at a moderate pace—no more than two to three pounds a week. If you see that you're dropping more than that each week, add some extra healthy food to your diet. It will help you learn to moderate your intake so you don't fall into the quick loss/regain patterns.

Don't skip meals.

Don't deny yourself. Have a small amount of something you really desire, a healthy cookie or extra serving of food. When possible, keep these splurges low fat.

Have a supportive friend to help you when you are feeling unmotivated and want to splurge. Sometimes all it takes is a caring friend to get fired up.

Exercise will decrease your appetite, lift your spirits, help burn extra fat, and increase your metabolic rate.

Avoid "diet" foods like sugar-free candies and low-cal frozen meals.

Eat your foods as close to the way nature made them as possible. Emphasize freshness, simplicity, variety, and wholeness.

My body is fit, trim, energetic, and healthy and is nurtured by my peaceful relationship with food.

Making Peace with Gravity

Gravity is the master of our environment; life is dominated by this universal force. Unhealthy foods, contaminated water, and polluted air can be avoided but you cannot get away from gravity. Gravity can have a negative effect on posture, skin tone, circulation, concentration, and all the organs of the body as it relentlessly pulls them down.

Work with gravity to improve your health. You can do this by slanting. Just a few minutes a day, lying with your head lower than your heart and your legs higher than your heart (some do this using a slantboard) can help reduce or eliminate headaches, insomnia, varicose veins, fatigue, neck and shoulder tension, and so much more. Slanting also improves posture, complexion, circulation, and fosters relaxation and peace of mind. Check out the terrific BodySlant (see *Resources*).

Every day I take time to relax
and find the peace of my own company.

Eating on the Go

Here are some ways to improve your diet and save time and calories while on the go.

Keep a zip lock bag with you filled with healthy delights like dried apricots, raw vegetables, or fresh fruit. Bring your lunch to work and don't skip lunch.

Don't go longer than three hours between meals or healthy snacks. Glucose, the brain's energy source, runs out in about five hours, forcing the body to use less-efficient fuel and compromising brain power.

Request that food be prepared to your liking. At a restaurant, ask that your entree be steamed, broiled, or grilled without butter, oil, or sauces. Stay away from fatty foods.

Keep healthy snacks in a drawer or office kitchen. Make sure you read the labels to ascertain the percentage of calories from fat. Choose only those snacks that have fewer than fifteen percent calories from fat.

Have several pieces of fresh fruit on an empty stomach each day. Fresh fruit gives you immediate energy, lots of nutrients, and a feeling of well-being.

Don't let your business meals be an excuse to binge. Focus on the business, not the food.

Dine, don't just eat. Make mealtime a pleasure, especially if your servings are smaller than usual.

I enjoying eating a variety of plant-based foods that are low in fat.

Tofu and Soybeans

Soybeans and many of the foods made from them such as tofu contain a variety of salutary compounds including *genistein,* which has been shown to inhibit a variety of cancers. Soybeans (and tofu) are the only dietary sources of genistein. Mori-Nu Silken "Lite" Tofu (see *Resources*) is the world's only low fat tofu with 75 percent fewer calories from fat than regular tofu. It has a creamy, silken texture that has made it so popular for American dishes. Use it in everything from soups and stir-fry to fruit shakes and low fat desserts. (See Day 41 for a terrific "Power Drink" that's easy to make in the blender.) A highly recommended cookbook with many tofu recipes is *Luscious Low Fat Desserts* by Marie Ozer. Mori-Nu uses no irradiation or preservatives in their tofu.

I look forward to my health and fitness program with enthusiasm and thanksgiving.

Steady Weight Gain Means Gaining Years

The majority of people who diet usually gain their weight back, and then some. Ralph Paffenbarger, M.D., of the Stanford University School of Medicine and I-Min Lee, M.D., at Harvard University School of Public Health, recently reviewed data on more than 30,000 male Harvard graduates to see how weight loss affects longevity. Their theory: losing weight means gaining years. Their surprise finding: people who shed pounds were just as much at risk of mortality as those who put on weight, while people who maintained a stable weight had less risk than both gainers and losers.

The epidemiologists discovered that people whose weight fluctuated during the eleven to fifteen-year study period had been experiencing the same cycle of losing weight only to gain it back again all their lives. Yo-yo dieting adversely affects longevity in two specific ways. During periods of weight loss or gain, the body's cholesterol levels increase, only subsiding after a stable weight is maintained. If you change your weight often your cholesterol never has a chance to level off, and may remain unhealthily high.

People who undergo cycles of weight loss and gain also tend to put the weight back on around the middle. Abdominal fat, like high cholesterol, is associated with an increased risk of mortality.

The best advice from the experts is to achieve a healthy weight and stay there, not just by eating sensibly but also by exercising more.

I weigh _____ pounds easily and effortlessly.
Being fit and trim is a way of life for me.

Acid-Alkaline Balance

The human body has what may be called an alkaline condition. This normal state of slight alkalinity (approximately 7.4 in the blood) is maintained by various mechanisms within the body's control. You may effectively aid the body in maintaining this condition by eating foods which predominated the alkaline-forming elements.

When food is metabolized, either an acid or an alkaline residue is left in the body, depending on which mineral elements are dominant. The acid-forming minerals are sulfur, phosphorus, and chlorine. The alkaline-forming ones are sodium, potassium, calcium, magnesium, and iron. Flesh foods (such as eggs), cheese, legumes, grains (except millet), nuts, and seeds can be classified as acid-forming. All fruit and most vegetables (sprouts included) are alkaline-forming.

To maintain the proper acid/alkaline ratio, the diet should consist of at least eighty percent alkaline-forming foods and not more than twenty percent acid-forming foods. When acid-forming foods are eaten, they should always be accompanied by a considerable quantity of vegetables to balance the meal, preserving the alkaline mineral reserves in the tissues. This is really where the emphasis should be placed when determining an appropriate balanced diet.

I choose to live a balanced life.

Fasting for Rejuvenation

A forty-year-old man can fast for three weeks and be restored to the physiological level of a seventeen-year-old. Where else can you find anything which will restore youthfulness? There is nothing else in the realm of nature that can accomplish this like fasting can.

There are several certified fasting clinics in the United States and elsewhere. It's important to be supervised when you undertake a fast, especially if it's your first time. In a certified fasting clinic, you are monitored and supervised every step of the way. When you join the American Natural Hygiene Society (see *Resources*), you'll receive the magazine *Health Science* which includes a listing of certified fasting clinics. If you've considered fasting before, now is the time to do it. You will reap great rewards physically, mentally, emotionally, and spiritually.

I take responsibility for my wellness lifestyle
and am open to new ways of being radiantly healthy
in body, mind, and spirit.

Sweating and Saunas

For thousands of years, people around the world have enjoyed the therapeutic benefits of saunas. Sweating is an important part of physical well-being, especially in the modern world. Water and airborne pollution, toxic chemicals, heavy metals, and poor dietary and exercise habits make internal cleansing by regular sweating critical to maintaining a healthy body and mind.

Only the most active athletes achieve prolonged sweating through exercise on a daily basis, and usually not of the deep type that will flush out toxins. Those who are unable to exercise heavily have an even greater need to create a regular sweat. Deep sweating through daily saunas is the best method for everyone to flush out accumulated poisons.

Soft Heat (see *Resources*) manufactures home radiant heat infrared saunas, the same type used by many doctors, physical therapists, and professional athletes. Make using a sauna an important part of your fitness program.

My body is truly a miracle of miracles.

Sweating and Saunas II

When saunas are used regularly, they improve blood circulation, toxin and heavy metal reduction, weight control, and skin cleansing, and reduce allergies, rashes, and muscle and joint pain.

Soft Heat (see *Resources*) manufactures saunas handcrafted from aromatic cedar wood that are low cost, energy efficient, and more effective than old technology saunas. The radiant heat infrared sauna warms the muscles directly, keeping the air temperature at a comfortable level, and allows for fresh air ventilation. This type of sauna has greater therapeutic results than high temperature saunas. The Health Mate sauna is made for personal or small group use and is sold complete requiring no assembly. It uses regular 110 volt household current and costs only pennies a day to operate.

Because a person is able to use this type of sauna for a longer time, there are greater benefits than from conventional saunas. The safe and UL approved radiant heat infrared technology is similar to that used by doctors and physical therapists to treat muscle injuries and by hospitals to warm newborn babies. Give yourself a daily sauna and see the difference it can make.

I celebrate the joy of living and I celebrate me.

Creating a Beautiful Home

Make your home a sanctuary. Whether you live in a mansion or an apartment, there are countless things you can do that will enrich the quality of your life. Don't feel compelled to fill up all the spaces. Space is a luxury and having pure space will give you a serene feeling. You will feel less anxious and more at rest and peace in a room that breathes with openness, like a refreshing walk in the country. Walk through your home today and see if there are ways you can simplify and create more breathing space.

Fill your spaces with things that give you joy and peace. Fresh flowers, natural baskets, light, beautiful colors on your walls, and great fragrances. Let every room bring you joy and peace. You don't have to have lots of money to create a sanctuary. Just do what feels right and peaceful to you. Paint a room, bring in some fresh plants, wash your windows, clean out some closets, and let go of what no longer serves you or brings you joy.

My home is my sanctuary
and is filled with love, peace, and joy.

Creating a Healthy Sex Life

To create a healthy sex life, you must be honest about what you like and don't like—and what you want and don't want. Lovers must communicate. Being open to sharing your fantasies and desires is probably the best way to keep sex fresh and exciting. Sex can continue to be great long after the newness of a relationship has diminished.

Communicate honestly about sex and other feelings. It's the distance that contributes to a loss of sexual excitement. The best time to let your lover know your wants and desires is over a candlelight dinner and chances are the conversation will result in a memorable night of loving.

I receive great pleasure in pleasuring my partner.
I love to be intimate and find
special ways to keep intimacy alive.

Be True to Yourself

Take a good, hard look at your life and take responsibility for everything. Seek truth and justice in your daily life. Don't let pride stand in the way of understanding and peaceful living. Allow others their truth even if it differs from yours.

Know that you are solely responsible for your actions and for your inner peace. Be grateful for this and all blessings. Remember that free will is the blessing that allows you to experience life in order to learn the lessons that lead to wisdom. It is often more difficult to be grateful for the uncomfortable lessons; they also allow you to grow when you take responsibility for your part. Look for the lesson in any challenge and the challenge dissipates. If you allow it, everything that happens to you is designed to teach holiness and bring you closer to God.

I am true to myself and grateful for all my life's lessons and oneness with God.

Peace Pilgrim

Peace Pilgrim was a walking, breathing example of living peacefully. For more than twenty-eight years, she traveled the length of North America, all fifty states, the ten provinces of Canada, and parts of Mexico sharing her thoughts about peace. Her journey was on foot, never asking for anything: food, shelter, or transportation. She walked without a penny in her pocket. All she had were the clothes she wore (pants, shirt, tennis shoes and a short sleeveless tunic lettered boldly on the front "Peace Pilgrim"). Her motto was as simple as her life: "This is the way of peace: overcome evil with good, and falsehood with truth, and hatred with love." There was only one thing that could inspire and support a journey of this extent and provide the strength to see it through for all those years, and that is absolute, uncompromising faith in herself and in God.

On peace, she said: "When you find peace within yourself, you become the kind of person who can live at peace with others. Inner peace is not found by staying on the surface of life, or by attempting to escape from life through any means. Inner peace is found by facing life squarely, solving its problems, and delving as far beneath its surface as possible to discover its verities and realities."

For a free book on Peace Pilgrim and her life and philosophy, see *Resources*.

*I live in a peaceful world
because I am a peaceful person.*

Setting Your Goals

To achieve your goals, be very clear about what you want. If you want to create more abundance in your life, decide on what amount of money you'd like to make a year. Write out your goal in clear and concise words. If you were living your highest vision for yourself right now, what would your life be like? Really think about this and write out your vision for every area of your life including career, health, relationships, and lifestyle. Add in what you want in terms of prosperity, creativity, peace, and spiritual matters.

After you have written down all of the things you have ever wanted to achieve, turn within and seek assistance from your inner guidance. It is always there to guide you but you must ask for help, pay attention, and then act on what comes to you. Let yourself receive the inner knowing that comes from being in tune with yourself. Times of daily solitude and meditation will make it much easier for you to be in tune with your inner guidance. Trust, believe, and have faith.

I place all my cares, worries, problems, and goals into the light of God and ask that only those things for my highest good be brought forward.

The Art of Living Beautifully

To feed your soul in everyday life, use your imagination to enrich the way you live. When you decorate your home, don't settle for someone else's taste. Your home should be your sanctuary and express your feelings, emotions, and imagination. Think about the location, furnishings, and decorations so they satisfy you emotionally and express your soul's individuality.

Always surround yourself with nature. Bring in plants and fresh flowers. Paint your walls colors that move and inspire you. Make sure there's quality music to enrich your life in the many rooms of your home.

Have a room, or a corner of a room, that's just for you — a meditation area where you visit daily to turn within to find the peace of your own company.

I see beauty all around me
because I see with God's eyes.

Consumer Beware

Use products with the least amount of chemicals and are the most natural for your body. Wear natural clothing made from either cotton, wool, or silk. Select home cleaning products that are safe for you as well as the environment.

Ultra-concentrated laundry detergents—liquid and powder—can burn the skin if used incorrectly. They may not wash out of fabrics completely. Perspiration can reactivate them, leading to chemical burns. Make sure you add your detergent after the machine fills with water and measure carefully. Don't put in too much. If a reaction occurs, take a cool shower, apply cool compresses, or call your doctor if it persists for more than a day.

Consider using detergents that are biodegradable and are free of perfumes and other unnecessary added ingredients.

*I select products in my home that are safe
for my body as well as Mother Earth.*

Releasing Anger

Of all the moods we experience, anger is often one of the hardest to shake. Here are some of the ways to lift yourself from an angry mood.

Exercise. As a result of the chemicals that are released in your body when you exercise, you will be in a more positive frame of mind and be able to see the situation from a higher perspective.

Talk to a friend you trust and with whom you feel safe. Friends can help you see things more clearly and help process your feelings.

Another way to defuse anger or even rage is to try to understand the motivation of the person who provoked it. Make a joke of the situation, as difficult as it might be, and don't take your life and circumstances so seriously.

Spend some time alone. Go out into nature and walk in a park, by the ocean, or take a hike. It's also nice to be pampered. Go get a facial, a manicure, or a great massage.

Put on some classical or other peaceful music or read an uplifting book.

*I release my fears and insecurities
and replace them with faith and confidence.*

Embrace Sunshine

The sun is important for radiant health. There are ways you can protect yourself from the harmful effects of too much sun. Beta-carotene, a vitamin abundant in spinach, carrots, cantaloupe, papaya, kale, endive, arugula, and romaine lettuce, has been found to be helpful in reducing the harmful effects of too much sun on the immune system.

Your body produces vitamin D from sunlight to be able to absorb calcium. Just ten minutes of walking on the sunny side of the street daily should minimize the risk of vitamin deficiency.

For insightful reading on the benefits of sunlight, read *Sunlight* by Zane Kime.

I give thanks for increasing health, love, prosperity, and vitality.

Keeping Passion Alive

Passion keeps relationships radiant and healthy. It's something that ebbs and flows between two people and needs attention and nurturing, like a garden needs watering and weeding to keep growing and alive.

The key to keeping the passion alive is communicating about and resolving all suppressed anger and hurt on a daily basis. Practice resolving conflicts when they are still small—avoiding little fights eventually causes bigger fights which are harder to resolve.

Give your partner a twenty second kiss three times a day—just enough to get the sexual attraction stirred up. Who says every time you get turned on you have to go all the way?

Spend five minutes at the end of each day expressing your gratitude with your partner for the day that has just passed, whether it's simply being grateful for the kiss in the morning, or the help in the kitchen.

As relationship expert and author of *Are You the One for Me?* Barbara DeAngelis suggests, be aware of the four R's: resistance, resentment, rejection, repression. They represent the four stages of the death of a relationship. Don't suppress the resistance because it will become resentment which builds up to rejection and turns into repression which signals the end of a relationship.

I communicate my feelings openly, lovingly,
and honestly with my partner and friends.

Aloneness

Find some time today and every day to be alone. Embrace and enjoy the peace of your own company. If you improve all the outside factors (including exercise, eating habits, your job), it will be of little value unless you also look inward for peace and harmony. By virtue of being a divine child of God, you already have everything you need to live your highest potential.

Henry David Thoreau wrote, "It is a great relief when for a few moments in the day we can retire to our chamber to be completely true to ourselves. It leavens the rest of our hours." And also, "I love to be alone. I never found the companion that was so companionable as solitude."

Take a few minutes to be alone and to find the peace of your own company. When you feel the peace that's always with you, you can then bring that peace to everything you do.

God's wisdom illuminates me,
filling my path with light.

Making a Difference

How you live and respond to other people can make a positive difference in their lives. Bring energy, love, and life into any room you enter.

People really like people who like them. If you show an interest in someone, he or she will be interested in you.

Recognize the need all people have to make a connection and to share something about themselves. It's really quite simple. Everyone just wants to be appreciated and loved for themselves.

I have something unique to offer.

Affirm the Life You Want

Affirmations are statements of truth about you or what you want to create. Repeated throughout the day, especially when you are going to sleep at night and just waking up in the morning, they are very powerful and effective. Here are a series of affirmations to support you in being all that you are capable of being.

I am a clear channel through which the love of the universe shines.

I love and accept myself completely, as I am.

I eat foods that nourish my body and soul.

My body is trim, fit, and beautifully-shaped.

I weigh exactly what I desire, easily, effortlessly, and consistently.

I exercise vigorously on a regular basis and I love it.

I am accountable and responsible for my own life and I celebrate life.

I choose to see problems as opportunities.

I create relationships that are loving, supportive, expressive, and alive.

I affirm the life I desire and deserve and surrender it all to God. My will and divine will are one.

Roadblocks to Happiness

"An obstacle is like a hurdle in a steeplechase—ride up to it, throw your heart over it, and the horse will go along, too." Obstacles in your path are a wonderful gift, if you choose to look at them that way. They teach you more about yourself and to look at things differently. Changing how you see things is really an attitude shift.

"Difficult" and "bad" are both judgments on a situation that could also be called change. You're really dealing with changing times. So with this change of attitude, instead of looking at the times in which we now live as troubled or difficult, choose instead to see moments of enormous opportunity. Maintain at all times an attitude of gratitude. That will do wonders in bringing more happiness and peace to your life.

See your life experiences as stepping stones for your road to success. It all depends on how you look at it.

I deserve to be happy, live fully, and celebrate life.

Cherish Your Books

Books are able to give great joy, satisfaction, and inspiration. Some you can read over and over and receive new insight with each reading. Those books you want to keep and reread and share, take loving care of them. Those you no longer have any use for, give away.

Store books vertically on shelves, away from direct light and in a well-ventilated area. Shelve books of the same size together so they can support one another and stack no more than three oversized books horizontally. Keep old books in custom-fitted boxes or on book cradles if displayed open. Preserve original dust jackets in plastic wrappers to add value to the book. You may even arrange books according to topic, or alphabetically by author or title as you'd find them in a library or bookstore.

I enjoy reading books that motivate, inspire,
and empower me.

Time Management

Whether you manage an office, company, or household, there's often a plethora of time wasters. Here are some ways to manage your time that are efficient and effective.

When you have a big project or priority task, carve out an hour or more of private time without interruptions. Choose the time you are the freshest.

Create private time by screening your calls. You can do this through a secretary, voice mail, or screening messages on your telephone answering machine. Let those around you know this is your time to be left alone. Put a sign up on your door and let others know they can leave a message if necessary. You may also consider leaving your office or home to secure more privacy.

Make your phone calls more productive. Open the conversation with "What can I do for you?" This gets you right to the point. Avoid telephone tag. Know your schedule and suggest the best time to reach you. Return calls near lunch time or the end of the day when people are less apt to chat. Set a specific phone or appointment date.

When someone comes to your home or office for a visit, stand up as if you were leaving and talk as you are walking them out the door, if you don't have time for a chat. If possible, set open times when others know it's okay to visit.

It's your time and a precious commodity.

I am the captain of my life.
My work is fulfilling and love in action.

Ritual and Ceremony

While change must be accepted as inevitable and usually for the best, you can still bring some measure of constancy into your life. Ritual and ceremony can provide a familiar consistency while the world around you may be in turmoil. Your relationships with other people as well as your higher power may be strengthened through ritual and ceremony.

In the past, religion, cultural, and family traditions provided ritual and ceremony. Today, often what remains of these is merely rote or habit, lacking any spiritual depth or deep meaning. The sacred holidays have become mere business ventures.

You can enrich and stabilize your life, relationships, and connection to a higher power through ritual and ceremony. Find ways to bring these into your life. You can choose from any culture, family tradition, or whatever to make rituals that are important to you and speak to your own special needs.

For some excellent reading on the topic, try *The Art of Ritual* by Renee Beck and Sydney Metrick, *The Magic of Ritual by* Tom R. Driver, and *Ceremonial Circle* by Sedonia Cahill and Joshua Halpern.

Everything about my body and my life is sacred to me.

The Meaning of Life

Life's meaning comes from within. What you feel is right for you is right for you. Use your energy and talents to focus on that internal vision and go after it. Know that true happiness can only be found inside you. Once you tap into your inner, never-ending fountain of happiness, you can carry that joy and delight to everything in your outer life. Once you realize that you are already enough, then everything will be enough. You'll stop searching and start living and being.

I am the writer, director, and actor of my own movie.
God is guiding me to fulfillment.

Attracting Love and Friendship

Whether you are interested in attracting a friend or lover, the important thing to remember is that you must first be that which you want to attract. Finding the right person is about being the right person. Attract love and friendship by learning to give love and be a friend. Accept love and friendship and know that you are worthy and deserving to have the best. Don't focus so hard on finding a mate that you forget the important people already in your life. Once you learn to love yourself, you'll be able to love others and believe you deserve to be loved yourself. When you do this, your own true love and special friend will appear in your life. Be open and be willing to give love and kindness to yourself and others.

When I love others, I love myself.

Smile More

Smiles indicate self-acceptance and the acceptance of others. Smiles inspire confidence in the person smiling, make people feel good about themselves, and are the shortest distance between two people.

Just because you are at work doesn't mean you can't be happy and smile. It makes your day more energetic and enjoyable when you work with a smile on your face. Smiling can also intimidate or confuse an adversary, soften the blow of bad news, and reduce tension in your body. You can build a reputation as a winner if you smile whether you win or lose. Start right now and put a smile on your face. Keep it there all day and night and you'll discover the whole world looks a lot brighter.

I am a channel for love and happiness.

Science and Prayer

For a decade, the Spindrift organization in Salem, Oregon, has scientifically studied the ability of prayer to affect the behavior of simple biological systems, like the germination rates of seeds, or the metabolic activity of yeast cultures. There was clear evidence that prayer exerts a power effect.

One of the most interesting findings of the Spindrift studies concerns the effect of different kinds of prayer. They have compared two prayer strategies, directed and non-directed. In directed prayer, the praying person attaches a specific outcome to the prayer. In contrast, non-directed prayer does not ask for a specific outcome, the praying person simply asks for the best to occur in any particular situation. What is best is left for God, the absolute, or the universe to decide. Which approach works best? The Spindrift studies show that, although both approaches are effective, the non-directed approach is much more powerful than the directed approach.

Spindrift researchers suggest that the reason non-directed prayer works better is because there may be an inherent perfection, wholeness, or "rightness" in the world that will manifest itself if all obstructions are removed. If so, one need not tell the universe what to do, for God knows already; God does not have to be given orders.

*Today I let go and let God's will be my will
in every area of my life.*

Your Immune System

Our immune system protects us every moment from illness. It is indispensable and usually awesomely effective. A number of scientists today believe that not only are many immune system problems related to stress, but that there is also an intimate connection between our thoughts, feelings, expectations, and our resistance to disease as well as our ability to heal ourselves.

You have probably had the experience of catching a cold when you were under stress. But you can probably also recall times when you felt very sure you would not get sick, even though a virus was running rampant in your community. Perhaps you felt that you simply could not afford to get ill because of a commitment you had made to a client, a project deadline, or because of a special date coming up. It was as if you asserted your will to keep going and your immune system responded capably.

Support your immune system by living a balanced life. Set priorities, take time to relax, and celebrate this miracle called life.

My mind is filled with thoughts of peace, love, and joy.

Being Responsible

If you want to live fully and peacefully, let go of anger and blame. Take responsibility for your life and the choices that you make consciously and unconsciously. Make a commitment to work towards forgiveness of yourself and others, and do whatever it takes to uncover the underlying causes for whatever is happening in your life. Taking responsibility requires changing your mindset to include the idea that you create your own reality. Everything that is happening to you is your own doing, though it may be unconscious. The thoughts and beliefs you hold are constantly producing the circumstances set before you.

You are a perfect child of God with a heart of love and goodness inside. That condition always exists regardless of what you do or say. The circumstances of your life are the most effective circumstances to heal your inner wounds. The universe always brings what is perfect for your highest good. Your lower personality self may not recognize this at the time, but in retrospect, you can look at painful events in your life that have moved you quite a distance in spiritual and emotional growth, away from fear or anger toward a greater state of peace.

I am the creator of my life and confident, self-assured, and optimistic about my life and future.

Finding Your Purpose

Everyone has a purpose; it is not really a goal that can be attained. Purpose is the direction your life is headed.

To find your purpose, all you need to do is to be still and listen to your inner guidance. Many people choose prayer to get answers; remember to listen for the answers. It is by sitting quietly and listening that the answers will come.

I am ready to release my inner barriers
to fulfill my purpose on earth.

Boosting Your Self-Esteem

How you feel about yourself affects all aspects of your life—whether you are happy, peaceful, successful, and fulfilled in life. Here are some of the key ingredients to loving yourself and thus making your life a celebration.

Take loving care of your body. Eat healthy foods and exercise regularly. Think of your body as more than pounds of flesh and tissue; treat your body as the miracle it is and with love and respect.

Count your blessings. Look at all the positive aspects about your body and life and write them down so you can see them all the time. Make a list of all the things for which you are grateful: your eyes which show you beauty, your hands which let you touch, your children, your spouse and friends, the flowers in your yard, or the park down the street.

Be patient and trust. Everything happens in the proper timing. Trust that all will unfold for your highest good. Be patient with yourself and choose to live one day at a time.

I like and value myself very much.

Boosting Your Self-Esteem II

Be here now. Live in the present moment and with as much love in your heart as possible. All you ever truly have is this present moment, your moment of power.

Let go of all criticism. Be loving and kind towards yourself and release all criticism. When you catch yourself being judgmental and critical, stop and think of something positive. At least once a day, look in your mirror and take one minute to praise and support yourself.

Be of service to others. One of the fastest ways to feel better about yourself is to do something nice for another person. It could be as simple as giving someone a hug, cooking a meal for a sick neighbor, giving your time watching a friend's child so he or she can have some time off, or sending a card saying how much you appreciate another. In giving to others, we give to ourselves.

Live in the presence of love. There is nothing that will transform your life more quickly than living with a consistent feeling of love in your heart. For the next twenty-four hours maintain a consistent feeling of love; your entire life will change for the better and will be enriched. It's not very easy. Keep practicing and see how long you can go.

I treat myself to the very best; I deserve it.

Learn to Relax

Elicit a relaxation response so that your stress level is under your control. Become deeply relaxed in body and mind by doing something that soothes and calms you. Learn some deep breathing and other deep relaxation techniques such as meditation, yoga, and visualization.

Get involved in sports and recreational activities. Pursue a hobby. These type of activities help you to live a more balanced life.

Part of the relaxation process is to rid yourself of negative emotions. Prolonged feelings of anger, depression, helplessness, and hopelessness trigger the release of substances that can suppress the immune system. Find a way to clear up your negative feelings as thoroughly and quickly as possible.

Make sure you get enough sleep. Find some time each day, just for yourself, to relax. Choose to live a balanced life.

My sleep is relaxing, rejuvenating, and refreshing.

Take Loving Care of Yourself

Unconditionally cherish, love, and respect your body temple, no matter what your current shape. Let your body be your friend; love it with tender, loving care. Although your body is but a temporary home for your spiritual being, still take care of it. Love your body and be committed to being the best you can be.

My body is truly a miracle of miracles.

The Greatest Secret

Life flows from the inside out. You are affected by what happens inside. You are affected by your own feelings, your own thoughts. Nothing outside has the power to affect you.

Your life is a reflection of your predominant feelings toward yourself. When you are bothered or annoyed by something another person does, look within yourself and see what you're doing that bothers or annoys you. When you admire a quality in another, appreciate a beautiful sunset or other gift of nature, be aware that you are also appreciating some beauty within you.

Next time you blame another person or anything else for how you feel or for what you are experiencing, stop and check yourself and remember this truth: what you feel or experience at any point in time is up to you. Change your thoughts and you change your life.

I dwell in the presence of God's eternal love.

Your Beliefs Create Your Reality

Your life is a duplication of the beliefs you hold. All that you have ever dreamed, desired, or thought is what you have at this very moment. If you desire some changes in your life, first you must change your beliefs, thoughts, and the words you speak.

Norman Cousins said, "The greatest force in the human body is the natural drive of the body to heal itself—but that force is not independent of the belief system, which can translate expectations into physiological change. Nothing is more wondrous about the fifteen billion neurons in the human brain than their ability to convert thoughts, hopes, ideas, and attitudes into chemical substances. Everything begins, therefore, with belief. What we believe is the most powerful option of all."

Let today be a new beginning of identifying and releasing all negative beliefs and embracing only those thoughts and beliefs which serve your highest self.

I have the power and ability to live my highest vision.
My life is in divine order.

The Wonders of Garlic

For over 5,000 years, garlic has acquired a world-wide reputation as a preserver and restorer of health and youth. But raw garlic and related preparations are chemically unstable and have been known to cause side effects when taken internally, such as stomach disorders and allergic reactions.

On the other hand, processed garlic is rich in a variety of sulfur-containing compounds which act synergistically to provide the benefits of garlic. An aged garlic extract called *KYOLIC* (see *Resources*) has been developed based on the traditional usage of garlic. Instead of using heat, *KYOLIC* is aged naturally for twenty months. The unique natural aging process adds greatly to the value of garlic: the harsh and irritating compounds are significantly reduced, the pungent odor of garlic is also reduced, and sulfur-containing compounds, such as alliin and allicin, are converted to many other sulfur-containing compounds, which are mainly water-soluble. *KYOLIC* Aged Garlic Extract has been studied extensively and shown to have almost all known garlic benefits without any side effects. Studies have shown *KYOLIC* to be effective in lowering of cholesterol, immune enhancement, heart diseases, infectious diseases, cancer, liver disease, and aging.

I turn to nature for health
and always treat myself with love and respect.

Keep the Muscle, Lose the Fat

Here are four steps to successful weight loss:
Reduce dietary fat consumption to no more than fifteen percent of your daily calories. Most of the fat in your body comes from dietary fat. Fat does little to control hunger or stimulate metabolism. Avoid fatty foods. To calculate the percentage of fat calories in a food, multiply grams of fat by nine and divide by total calories.

Increase dietary fiber—low in calories, high in nutrients. High intakes of fiber have a bulking effect that helps to control hunger. Emphasize whole grains like brown rice, beans, and oatmeal, and fresh fruit and vegetables.

Get regular exercise and burn fat calories. Aerobic exercise burns calories and weight training increases your lean muscle tissue and your metabolic rate while also enhancing your body's capacity to burn fat. Exercise at least three times weekly for at least thirty minutes per session and choose aerobic exercises that engage legs and hips in continuous motion such as jogging, cycling, stair climbing, brisk walking, or skating. Exercise is essential for long term weight loss.

Visualize your body the way you'd like it to be. In your mind's eye, see yourself healthy, lean, and fit and feel those emotions of joy and thanksgiving you would feel if this vision were your current reality. Henry David Thoreau said, "The world is but a canvas to your imagination."

My healthy lifestyle is an inspiration to my family and friends.

Fresh Fruits

All fruits are good for you but some fruits are better than others. The Center for Science in the Public Interest ranked thirty-nine fruits, assigning points based on their amounts of vitamins A and C, potassium, and other nutrients, plus fiber. Topping the list was papaya. Pears canned in juice scored lowest (canning destroys pears' already low vitamin C content). Eat two to four fruit servings daily; a serving is one half cup or one medium fruit. Here are the top twelve.

FRUIT	SERVING SIZE	CALORIES
Papaya	1/2	59
Cantaloupe	1/4	47
Strawberries	1 cup	45
Orange	1	62
Tangerines	2	74
Kiwi	1	46
Mango	1/2	68
Apricots	4	68
Persimmon	1	118
Watermelon	2 cups	100
Raspberries	1 cup	61
Grapefruit	1/2	37

*I am energetic and enthusiastic
about my healthy lifestyle.*

Eliminating Dairy Products

Milk was once thought a wholesome and nat-ural food. Today there's new evidence that milk and all dairy products are harmful to your health. When you give up eating dairy foods, your health will greatly improve with more energy, feeling lighter, and no more sinus problems.

Most people aren't aware of the plethora of chemicals, hormones, antibiotics, and other drugs which are given to cows to fatten them up and make them produce more milk. Forty-five million people in the United States alone visit doctors each year to receive treatment for symptoms of dairy allergies such as asthma, eczema, hay fever, and lactose intolerance (the inability to digest milk sugar). What's more, heart disease (the leading cause of death in the United States) has been linked to excessive commercial dairy product consumption, as are digestive disorders, glandular disturbances, arthritis, allergies, cavities, and more.

Instead of dairy, why not try making nut milk?

I love and respect my body
and feed it the best foods possible.

Nut Milks

Nut milks are an excellent replacement for dairy products. You can use a variety of nuts and seeds to make milks, ice cream, shakes, dips, and dressings.

Almond milk

      3 1/4 cups warm water
      1/3 cup organic raw almonds
      1 tbs. Omega-Life fortified flax seed
        (see *Resources*)
      1 tsp. lecithin granules
      2 tbs. sweetener (pure maple syrup)

In a two-quart saucepan, heat approximately 3 1/4 cups of pure water to almost boiling. Turn stove off and allow to sit.

Select and gather refrigerated fresh nuts and flax seed. Place the nuts in a grinder (or blender). Grind to a fine powder. Transfer the mixture to a blender.

To your blender add flax seed, lecithin granules, and sweetener. Then add 3/4 cup of the warm water and blend on medium speed to a smooth, pudding-like puree. Add the remaining water and blend on high speed until creamy. Use approximately three cups water per recipe for extra creamy nutmilks.

Pour the contents of the blender through a fine mesh strainer into a bowl or pitcher. Serve immediately or refrigerate for up to seventy-two hours. It's delicious when you blend in fresh fruit or a frozen banana.

My body is God's gift to me
and what I'm becoming is my gift to God.

Yoga

The most ancient of all fitness systems, yoga has many benefits. Yoga can increase lung capacity and height, aid digestion and circulation while reducing stress, insomnia, back pain, and asthma attacks. New studies show it can even help to reverse heart disease.

Hatha yoga (physical yoga, as opposed to meditative or devotional) is a system of breathing exercises and postures (asanas). Some poses may look contortionistic, but they can be modified for any body. It's the content—breathing and inner awareness—that's vastly more important than the form.

In yoga, the diaphragm (a floor for the heart and lungs; a ceiling for the liver, stomach, and spleen) is retrained to move vertically, thus massaging the adjacent vital organs and stimulating digestion and circulation. Yoga is also a stress buster, offering a respite in fast-paced American life, a way to quiet down and work on your body from the inside out.

It does require instruction. Check out dance studios, wellness centers, colleges, fitness clubs, and back clinics for classes. Find the right teacher for you. You may also consider a video program. There are some great ones available at your video store.

*My body is stress-free
because I take time each day to relax, turn within,
breathe deeply and let go of all tension.*

Staying Young

A recent study suggests that baby boomers may not have to rely on injections of human growth hormone to compensate for age-related declines in their later years. Researchers found that people in their sixties who had exercised regularly for most of their life had higher levels of the muscle-building, skin-toning hormone than sedentary people in their twenties.

Exercise can also alleviate some of the undesirable symptoms of menopause. Two recent studies have documented a reduction in hot flash severity in women who work out (one study involved runners; the other, women in an aerobic conditioning program). Exercise increases endorphin levels, which ultimately works to counteract, at least in part, the decreasing levels of estrogen and progesterone hormones, which can cause hot flashes and other symptoms in menopausal women.

Exercise, by improving mood and relieving stress, also alleviates fatigue, depression, tension, insomnia, and irritability that may accompany the change of life. It also counters the tendency to gain weight.

Every day I become fitter, stronger, and healthier.

Less Is More

The less fat you consume, the greater the volume of food you can consume for the same number of calories. Here are some examples:

For a fast-food breakfast, about 440 calories: instead of a cinnamon Danish with twenty-one grams of fat, have two and a half fat-free apple bran muffins.

From the toaster, for 210 calories: instead of a blueberry toaster pastry with six grams of fat, try three slices of whole-grain toast with two teaspoons of no-sugar blueberry preserves (all this has about three grams of fat).

At break time, for about 235 calories: instead of that glazed doughnut with thirteen grams of fat, have a small blueberry muffin and a banana for about three grams of fat total.

Anyway you slice it, you get to eat more with low fat choices, which makes for easier weight control and will improve your health.

Healthy foods are very appealing to me.
I choose to express radiant health.

The Grace of Eating

Throughout human history, mealtimes were a time when all the members of a family or group would gather. This was a time they could become one. They would share the day's experiences and nourish relationships. Food wasn't taken for granted and often a chant or prayer of thanksgiving was given prior to eating. Today everything seems to be rushed, even our meals. Often there is no time to eat together as families. Even singles and couples seem to prefer "fast food."

There is a transformation that happens to food when it is blessed. Studies have shown that water changes when infused with thoughts of love. It not only tastes sweeter but there's also a change in the oxygen and hydrogen bonds. If food and mealtimes were treated with more sacredness, there would be less disease and more healing.

Next time you sit down to a meal, pay attention. Notice every texture, flavor, and nuance of the food as you eat slowly and deliberately. If you make mealtimes more sacred and focus your thoughts on love and gratitude, your food will give greater nourishment. For some insightful and inspiring reading in this area, a highly recommended book is *May All Be Fed* by John Robbins.

I bless my food, my family, and this world.

Stress Buster: Side Stretch

Next time you feel anxious and tense, change your state of mind by stretching your body. You can even do this while sitting at your desk. Here's an easy exercise stretch designed to combat tension in the muscles that run along the side of your back.

Sit up straight in your chair with arms raised toward ceiling. Grasp your left wrist with your right hand, then smoothly and gradually pull the wrist up and over your head as far as you comfortably can. Hold the stretch for about twenty seconds. Relax and breathe evenly. Gently repeat the exercise three times on each side, trying to reach a little farther each time.

I let go and rest in the confidence
that I am a child of God.

Exercising Outdoors

If you exercise, chances are some of your activities will be outdoors. Here are some guidelines to keep you protected while you workout.

Don't exercise on traffic-filled roads; however, if this is your only choice, avoid peak traffic hours (which will also be easier on your lungs).

Walk or run against the flow of traffic on the road; cycle and skate with it.

Watch out for opening car doors or cars coming out of intersections, driveways, and parking spots.

Always wear a helmet when you skate or cycle. Bicycle helmets reduce the chance of brain injury by eighty-eight percent and could help prevent seventy-five percent of all bicycle-related deaths each year.

Carefully plan your route. Exercise in familiar areas that are well-populated and well-lit; have a variety of routes so no one can assume you'll pass by the same spot every day.

Carry identification and coins in case you need to make a phone call.

Always trust your instincts about a person or an area. If you feel uncomfortable, leave immediately.

I love to be outdoors
to celebrate God's beauty in nature.

How to Prevent Constipation

Difficult or infrequent bowel elimination is disagreeable enough, but it may also produce such troublesome symptoms as irritability, moodiness, depression, bad breath, fatigue, coated tongue, and headaches. To help your intestines return to normal, avoid low-fiber foods like white flour products, white sugar and heavily processed foods, and fatty foods like milk, hard cheeses, eggs, and red meats.

Make sure you have high-fiber whole foods, grains, such as brown rice, oats, corn, and barley (especially in a stew with vegetables). Also make sure your daily diet includes vegetables like kale, broccoli, carrots, and cauliflower and an abundance of fresh fruit.

Drink adequate amounts of water, approximately eight eight-ounce glasses daily.

Chew every mouthful thoroughly. Digestion begins in the mouth, and swallowing incompletely chewed foods puts a burden on your digestive system. For an effective laxative, make a compote of figs, prunes, and raisins. Start with 1/3 cup of each. Cut figs and prunes into small pieces. Place in a saucepan with raisins and cover with two pints of boiling water. Let sit for an hour or two and eat 1/2 cup in the morning.

Walk daily. Studies have consistently shown that exercise speeds the movement of food through the intestines and strengthens bowel function. Massage the lower abdomen in a clockwise motion.

The healthy foods I eat keep my digestive system running efficiently. I am grateful for the inherent wisdom of my body.

The Joy of Fruits

Fruits are nature's most superb creation for nour-ishment. In a state of perfect ripeness, they are unsurpassed as a complete delight to sensory appeal. There are more varieties of fruits than any other form of food. Eat fresh fruit on an empty stomach, and also take one day every week or two and have only fruit for the entire day. It provides a great cleansing to the entire body.

Fruits provide the body with rich sources of vitamins and minerals. They also contain small, yet adequate amounts of protein and fat, and their sugars provide the best source of easily assimilated carbohydrates. An important consideration of fruit eating is that it should be eaten in its ripened state, otherwise it may cause distress from not being properly digested.

More than other products of the soil, fruits receive the beneficial influences of light, heat, and air, through which the electric and magnetic forces of the sun are transmitted. Fruits have the highest rate of atomic cell vibrations of all foods, and while we cannot determine by chemical analysis this subtle power, we can feel, when eating fruits, their enlivening effects through our whole system.

I am grateful for nature's abundance
of delicious, nutritious fruits.

Health-Providing Foods

Sunflower Seeds: Similar to nuts in polyunsatu-rated fat content, but with much more vitamin E—the antioxidant that fights cancer, heart disease, and cataracts. An intake of at least 100 IU a day has been shown to have the greatest benefit (the RDA is currently 15 IU). Make sure you eat only those seeds which are raw and unsalted. Because of their high fat content (even though it's a healthy fat), you don't want to overdo them. Eat them regularly but sparingly.

Black Beans: Make a big batch of black beans to eat throughout the week. A bonanza of soluble fiber, the kind that helps lower LDL by as much as twenty-four percent and reduce blood pressure. The fiber also helps keep blood sugar levels on an even keel, staving off hunger, even reducing the need for insulin among diabetics. Other beans and peas are full of fiber, too.

Mango: Brimming with beta-carotene and vitamin C, the anticancer antioxidants, plus vitamin B6 and copper. Another health benefit of vitamin C is it helps lower blood pressure.

Kale: Another boon against heart disease, this under appreciated cruciferous vegetable is especially rich in carotene and vitamin C, both of which may reduce the harmful effects of LDL cholesterol. Kale is also packed with fiber, vitamin B6, copper, manganese, potassium and lots of calcium. Steam or juice kale and make sure you get a couple servings of it weekly.

I am sizzling with enthusiasm and vitality.

Life-Lengthening Vitamin

A ten-year study of more than 11,000 Americans aged twenty-five to seventy-four by James Enstrom, Ph.D., of the Jonsson Comprehensive Cancer Center at UCLA, has shown men who took at least fifty milligrams of vitamin C a day in their diets, and also daily multivitamin and/or vitamin C supplements, had a forty-one percent lower total mortality rate and six-year greater life expectancy than men whose diets provided less than fifty milligrams of vitamin C. The death rate from heart disease and stroke was forty-five percent lower among high-C than low-C men. Women also appear to benefit from the vitamin to a lesser degree.

The best-known sources of vitamin C are the citrus fruits—oranges, lemons, limes, tangerines, and grapefruit. The fruits with the highest natural concentrations are citrus fruits, rose hips, and acerola cherries, followed by papayas, cantaloupes, and strawberries. Good vegetable sources include green and red peppers (the best), broccoli, Brussels sprouts, tomatoes, asparagus, parsley, dark leafy greens, cabbage, and sauerkraut.

Each day I choose to eat several servings of vitamin C-rich fruits and vegetables.

Toddlers' Eating Patterns

Children often go through periods during which they insist on eating the same foods day after day. The reason is that toddlers need to establish comforting routines. Food jags or fads will not cause starvation or malnutrition and will, if ignored, usually run themselves out. In the meantime, continue offering a variety of nutritious foods at every meal, as well as healthy between-meal snacks. Don't try to force a child to eat different foods. This results in a no-win battle of wills and may cause them to develop a negative association between food and mealtime.

For more information on the best foods for toddlers and children, read *Dr. Attwood's Low-Fat Prescription for Kids* by Charles Attwood, MD, and my book co-authored with Dianne Warren, *Vegetable Soup/The Fruit Bowl.*

I feast on positive words and ideas.
I fast from negative thinking.

Lowering Blood Pressure

Exercise can be a potent remedy for mildly elevated blood-pressure levels. It's very common for doctors to first prescribe moderate exercise like walking, along with weight control, salt restriction, and stopping smoking—instead of drugs—to lower mildly elevated blood pressure. Exercise can lower elevated systolic and diastolic blood pressure by an average of ten points. That's enough to keep some people from ever having to take hypertensive medications. And some people who are already on blood pressure medications can reduce their doses or come off the drugs completely with those lifestyle changes.

The typical exercise prescription for hypertensives is thirty to forty-five minutes of brisk walking or other aerobic exercise, like stationary cycling, four or five days a week. Scientific evidence supporting resistance training as effective in lowering blood-pressure is mounting, too. Doctors still caution against lifting heavy weights if you have high blood pressure, though. That's because intense weight lifting can cause dangerous spikes in blood pressure. Most of the evidence indicates that circuit training may be the best and safest way of using resistance training if you have high blood pressure. When you circuit train, you lift light-to-moderately heavy weights using a number of different weight lifting machines, moving quickly from station to station.

If you have high blood pressure, check with your doctor before you adopt any exercise program.

When I feel the pressures of life, I take time out to slow down and turn within to the wonderful peace of God.

Exciting Beta-Carotene Studies

Heart Disease and Stroke: Scientists have found that women who ranked in the top fifth in beta-carotene intake had a twenty-two percent reduction of risk of heart disease and stroke.

AIDS: Researchers at the Oregon Health Sciences University studied twenty-one HIV-positive patients who were given 180 mgs. of beta-carotene every day for four weeks. They found the nutrient boosted the levels of infection-fighting white blood cells.

Skin Damage: Harvard researchers learned that beta-carotene increases the amount of time it took volunteers to develop a sunburn.

Cervical Cancer: Australian researchers studying the effects of beta-carotene on 218 women with cervical dysphasia, a pre-cancerous condition, found a lower-than-expected progression of the condition to cervical cancer among women taking the nutrient.

Lung Cancer: A University of Texas-based study of 149 patients with lung cancer and 359 people who were cancer-free found that those individuals with lung cancer had a lower intake of beta-carotene than those who were free of the disease.

My body is an expression of my love for life.
I radiate youthfulness.

Cancer-Diet Connection

In a research study by the Washington State Department of Health, it was reported that women who consumed greater quantities of vitamin C, folic acid, and lycopene were one-fifth as likely to develop cervical intraepithelial neoplasia, a condition that generally leads to cervical cancer. Best sources of vitamin C: citrus fruits, strawberries, cantaloupe, broccoli, tomatoes. Best sources of folic acid: whole grains, fruits and vegetables. Best sources of lycopene: tomatoes and other red or reddish foods, such as red peppers and ruby-red grapefruit. Lycopene is actually condensed when tomatoes are processed, so foods with tomato sauce are also good sources.

Embrace a diet high in fiber, low in fat, and that includes plenty of fresh fruit and vegetables daily.

My diet reflects my commitment
to radiant health and living fully.

Making Time to Exercise

Make exercise a regular part of your wellness lifestyle. In a study done at Harvard University, researchers looked at the physical activity levels of more than 17,000 men before and after an eleven-to-fifteen year period. They found that men who were moderately to highly active at both the beginning and end of the study were half as likely to develop colon cancer as inactive men.

On a regular basis, make time to exercise—either after work or early in the morning. It's important for staying motivated to exercise that you don't consider your exercise time to be lost family time. Instead look at it as a way to significantly improve the quality of family time by making you a healthier, more positive, and less stressed-out person.

Remember, make time for wellness.

I look forward to planning and participating in my daily exercise program.

Living Foods

Living foods can be described as being raw foods which have not been cooked, processed, or sprayed with pesticide or herbicide. These foods bring with them the highest level of nutrition and energy to build, fuel, cleanse, rejuvenate, heal, and optimize your level of well-being. When whole, live foods are fed to animals, their endurance is two to three times greater than if fed with the same foods after they have been cooked.

Thorough cooking destroys the ecological balance of the food. It destroys all of the food enzymes, makes half of the protein unavailable, destroys sixty to seventy percent of the vitamins, up to almost all of the B12, and inactivates many of the lesser factors like gibberellins, anthocyanins, nobelitin, and tangeretin which boost the immune system and other body functions. Cooking foods also disrupts the bio-electrical structure, the electroluminescence and the zeta potential of the food. All of these factors are important for building and maintaining our life force energy.

Strive to eat at least half of your diet raw and also do some reading on the topic of nutrition and raw foods; an excellent book is *Conscious Eating* by Gabriel Cousens, MD.

I select foods that provide my body with vitality and optimum nutrition. Raw foods are my favorite foods and I make them a majority of my daily diet.

Why Weight?

Many people have the misconception that just by skipping meals you'll lose weight. Initially you might but skipping meals, especially over several days, will lower your metabolic rate and cause you to gain weight on fewer calories when you start eating again. Strive to eat four or five smaller meals a day if you want to lose weight. Studies show that a 150-lb woman who eats three meals a day burns 150 calories more than a woman of the same weight who eats only two meals daily. Eating more often is essential for weight loss.

The important thing to consider is what you eat. Fruits, vegetables, and salads are excellent choices. Fruits are easy to digest and give quick energy. Salads and vegetables are high in fiber and nutrients and also low in calories. (Just watch out for those fat-rich dressings.)

As you increase your vitamin and mineral consumption through these low calorie foods, you should also notice that many of your cravings disappear or lessen. Mineral shortages can cause certain cravings. For example, a deficiency in the mineral chromium can cause a craving for sweets. So don't skip meals. When you are hungry, just make your meals low in calories and high in fiber and nutrients.

If you want to lose weight, you must include regular exercise in your wellness lifestyle. Aerobic exercise (jogging, stepping, cycling, brisk walking) burns the fat. Weight training will tone, define, and reshape your body. Go for it. Don't wait.

I am strong in my resolve
to be healthy, happy, and radiantly alive.

Which Spread Is Best?

A recent study at the USDA research laboratory showed that margarine can promote an increase in blood cholesterol, the precursor to coronary heart disease. How can margarine, a vegetable oil product, cause blood cholesterol to rise?

The problem is the processing. Margarine is made by converting vegetable oils from their natural liquid state into hydrogenated fats that are solid or semi-solid at room temperature. The hydrogenation process transforms the oils' naturally fluid cis-fatty acids into an unnatural trans-form. It is these trans-fats, found in processed foods, that wreak havoc in the blood.

A research project conducted in 1987 by the Harvard School of Public Health, analyzed the diets of 85,000 nurses over a period of eight years. Those with the highest intake of trans-fats showed greater risk for heart disease. Not only does a diet of trans-fats invite cardiovascular failure, it also increases the opportunity for immune-related diseases, because trans-fats affect immune response by lowering B-cell response and causing T-cells to proliferate.

Instead of using butter or margarine, try Spectrum Spread (see *Resources*), available in the refrigerator section of your health food store. It's a delicious non-dairy, no cholesterol substitute.

Changing diets for a healthier lifestyle means a commitment to discovering new ways of eating and cooking.

I radiate health and energy and express vitality.

Desert Succulent

Ka The aloe "cactus," actually a desert succulent, has been touted as one of the "miracle" green plants-and there is now good research to back many of the claims. The leaf gel (the inside of the leaf) and whole leaf juices can be used for treatment, both internally and externally.

The most common use of aloe vera is the application of its gel for burns, minor cuts, insect bites, skin irritations and as a skin moisturizer. Recent research shows that aloe vera also helps to alleviate ulcers, protects the gastrointestinal lining, has strong anti-inflammatory properties, and even antiviral and mild pain-relieving properties.

I drink Aloe Falls brand aloe juices because they are preservative-free, certified active, and even taste good (which is rare for aloe vera juices). The Aloe Falls plants are grown without herbicides or pesticides, and they produce the only aloe vera juices I have seen without preservatives. For more information, see *Resources*.

I love to exercise and choose to let nothing interfere with my commitment.

Healthy Foods

When you eat foods in their natural, fresh state, you receive more nutrients and a greater benefit for your body. Plant-based foods contain an abundance of vitamins, minerals, enzymes, and fiber, all necessary ingredients for a healthy body.

Brussels sprouts, corn, zucchini, pinto and lima beans, cauliflower, and fresh currents all have as much cholesterol-lowering soluble fiber as does cooked oatmeal. A potato has almost double the potassium of a banana. And ounce for ounce, kale contains more calcium than milk. Red peppers have almost one and a half times more vitamin C than green peppers, and almost eleven times as many carotenoids. Ounce for ounce, cauliflower has more vitamin C than oranges. In fact, just one cup of cauliflower delivers more than the recommended daily allowance of vitamin C.

Most fruits ripen faster when left in a plastic or paper bag, since the bag traps the ethylene gas that is produced by the fruit and acts as a ripening agent. Apples give off large amounts of gas, so you can help speed the ripening of other fruits by placing an apple or apple slices in the bag with them.

Reduce your salt intake. Don't be fooled into thinking sea salt is better. By the time unrefined sea salt is processed for the table, it is almost identical to regular salt. For better health, eliminate all table salt from your diet. You can substitute herbs if you wish.

I am delighted to be healthy, vibrant,
and filled with joy and thanksgiving.

Variety in Your Diet

Make your food selection as close to its natural, God-created state as possible. The nutritional value is higher in these foods. Food should be whole and fresh. Choose brown rice over white refined rice, a whole orange over a processed orange fruit drink, whole baked potatoes over french fries or potato chips.

Strive to eat at least half of your foods raw. Raw foods provide more vitamins, minerals, enzymes, fiber, and bulk because they are "live" foods at the peak of nutritional value, if properly selected.

Also, select a diet that is eighty percent alkaline and twenty percent acid. Basically, most fresh vegetables and fruits (including citrus) are alkaline while grains, legumes, and animal products are acid. Emphasis on alkaline foods boosts your immune functioning and promotes radiant health. For simplicity, each day have six vegetables (two of which are leafy greens), at least two fruits, one starch, one protein, and at least one variety of sprouts. Fruits are high in natural sugars and vitamins, starch is for energy, protein is for cell growth and repair, and the fibers in grains, fruit, and vegetables provide bulk. This is a winning combination to prevent and alleviate disease and promote high level wellness.

I am committed to being healthy, happy, peaceful, and prosperous.

Reduce Your Fat Intake

A diet high in fat is very detrimental to your health. A high fat diet causes clogged arteries, high blood pressure, fatigued hearts, and heart attacks. It clumps red blood cells, causing slower blood flow to the brain and all tissues. This type of diet impairs function of the liver, slows digestion, and also slows the mind because of sluggish circulation. In addition, it zaps energy, decreases endurance/athletic performance, and diminishes sexual desire.

So now you're probably convinced that you'd like to cut back on your fat intake. How do you do this? Eat primarily low fat foods like vegetables, fruits, and grains. Meet your daily oil and fatty acid needs with unprocessed, uncooked whole foods such as raw seeds, nuts, and avocados and only eat these sparingly. Avoid fatty foods which have been cooked, fried, hydrogenated, or irradiated. Also avoid cooked foods with high fat content such as flesh foods, eggs, fried foods, dairy, mayonnaise, ice cream, pizza, cookies, and candies. Finally, avoid a high salt diet because it creates a craving for fats.

The foods I eat reflect how I feel about myself.
I love myself and want only the best for me.

Good Health Habits

Today is a wonderful opportunity to start fresh and commit to a new program of health, fitness, and living fully. Don't wait any longer. Embrace a wholesome lifestyle that supports you in living your highest potential.

Nutrition and exercise are essential ingredients for optimum health and living fully, but there are other equally important elements. These include deep breathing, fresh air, sunshine, pure water, and periodic fasting. Don't forget a positive attitude of forgiveness toward yourself as well as others, and releasing of negative emotions. To this list also add visualization, affirmations, simplifying your life, learning to relax, and becoming more childlike. Last, but not least, be sure to incorporate meditation, times of daily solitude, loving yourself unconditionally, and living more from inner guidance.

Don't wait any longer. Take charge of your life and choose to live fully.

I am the master of my life
and have the power to create anything I desire.

A Moving Experience

The colon has long been recognized as a key to overall physical health. As one of the most extensive detoxification organs of the body, its condition dramatically affects an individual's physical and psychological well-being. A healthy colon efficiently eliminates toxins, congestion, excessive mucus, and digested wastes, allowing the other organs of the body to function at their optimum with less stress.

A fiber-enriched diet, regular exercise, and adequate fluid intake generally contribute to a healthier colon. When the elimination system becomes unbalanced with constipation or irregularity and a restorative cleansing is desired, using a water-soluble fiber combination such as psyllium seed and husks can help promote comfortable bowel elimination which will assist the detoxifying process. Small amounts of herbs and natural bentonite clay complement the formula. Though categorized as a bulk-forming laxative, psyllium fiber works quite differently and more naturally than stimulating chemicals. Remember that sufficient intake of fluids is essential for maximum effectiveness.

My body naturally eliminates toxins
and rejuvenates itself.

Being Physically Active

To be radiantly healthy, exercise regularly. Exercise builds confidence, improves your immune system, lifts your spirits, alleviates depression, helps you to lose or maintain weight, tones your body, and reduces stress.

Exercise also increases your metabolic rate, especially if you lift weights and develop more lean muscle tissue. Muscle mass can shrink as people age and tend to become less active. This causes the body to burn less energy, and metabolism may decline by as much as ten percent per decade. The solution: eat less fat and increase exercise habits. Make exercise a part of your wellness lifestyle and a top priority in your life.

I keep all my agreements
and make only those agreements that I can keep.

Keeping Your Love Life Alive

No matter how long you've been in a relation-ship, it's important to explore ways of expressing your love sexually. Regardless of how sexually experienced you may be, there is always more to learn. Explore new possibilities and new ways of expressing your love with your partner. Keep the romance at high levels and always be a romantic at heart.

Being open to considering anything your partner suggests in making love allows for wonderful possibilities. Try different positions, times of day, and places, and don't suggest the same way all the time. By respecting each other's desires (as well as any reservations), you can continue to enrich your love life.

If you want your partner to do something different sexually, you'll be more likely to get them to agree by saying what you like than by focusing on what you don't like. Better still, change your own behavior in a way that might cause a change in your partner's behavior.

I create romance in my life by living lovingly.
I am lovable and feel good about being close.

Choose to See Beauty Everywhere

It's wonderful to be out in nature and to delight in her beauty. But you don't have to be in nature to see beauty all around you. If you keep your thoughts high and your heart pure, you will see beauty all around you everyday. You can see beauty in your work, while driving, when visiting or talking with others, and in even the most common things. When your heart is filled with love, or God, beauty is your constant companion.

> With beauty before me,
> May I walk
> With beauty behind me,
> May I walk
> With beauty above me,
> May I walk
> With beauty below me,
> May I walk
> With beauty all around me,
> May I walk
> Wandering on a trail of beauty,
> Lively, I walk.
>
> —Navajo chant

I walk in beauty with love and peace in my heart.

Nurturing Your Inner Child

It's easy to lose the joy of living when you take life and yourself too seriously. Life is to be celebrated and to be lived with enthusiasm. Sometimes the pressures of family, business associates, or friends will put you in a role that may cause great challenges. If you can lighten up a bit and try to see the bright side of every situation, you will move through those challenges and pressures more quickly. When you become too serious, your inner child goes into hiding and you can lose your zest for living. Give your inner child permission to come out and play and enliven your day.

If you've been too serious lately, why not dance in the rain, catch raindrops in your mouth, and walk barefoot on the grass; go to the circus, the park, or playground, swing on a swing, ride a merry-go-round, or spend some time with young children; laugh at yourself a few times every day; play hide and seek, pour water on a friend on a hot day, and go kiss a tree.

*I trust in the innocence, wonder, and aliveness
of my inner child and give it permission
to come out and enliven my day.*

Brother Lawrence

There's a special little book called *The Practice of the Presence of God* by Brother Lawrence. His simple message reflects the purity and directness of his approach to God. "He is nearer to us than we are aware of."

Brother Lawrence was a member of the Carmelite monastery in Paris in the mid 1600s. Most of his work was in the monastery kitchen; he writes, "The time of business does not differ with me from the time of prayer, and in the noise and clatter of my kitchen, while several persons are at the same time calling for different things, I possess God in as great tranquillity as if I were upon my knees at the blessed sacrament."

The secret of his work, he said, was always "pleasing myself by doing things to please God." He was a true lover of God and he often shared with others, "I am doing what I shall do through all Eternity—blessing God, praising God, adoring God, giving Him the love of my whole heart. It is our one business, my brethren."

I live in the peace of God.

Awakening Your Senses

Wake up to the joy, wonder, and magic all around you. A good way to help you to begin is to ask yourself these questions.

Are you living your highest vision now?

What changes would you like to see in your life?

Are you ready for some excitement that could very well mean the birth of a new you?

Acknowledge that desire as a goal you can accomplish. Begin your new quest in living your highest vision. Write out that vision and see yourself living that way. Affirm and expect your vision and act as if it were your reality now. Create your own vision quest. Go somewhere out in nature and pay attention to what the birds, trees, clouds, and flowers are saying to you. If you believe and pay attention, you will receive messages that will assist you on your way. Fire up your passion for life by believing that you have the power and ability to do and be anything you want. You must believe and trust.

And most importantly, surrender everything in your life over to God.

*My highest vision is rushing to me now
and I have a great passion for life.*

Etiquette Guidelines

Return calls and answer letters promptly. Calls should be returned within forty-eight hours and letters within two weeks. If you cannot respond within that time, have someone else do it for you.

Telephone etiquette. When you call someone and your call-waiting signals, ignore it. You made the call, so you should give it priority. Be respectful of a person's schedule and obligations when choosing a time to call.

Know how and when to apologize. Always make your apology as soon as possible after the event. Some acts require only a spoken apology, others require a spoken and written apology, and some require much more.

Write thank you notes for gifts, favors, meals, or any act of kindness. Also write notes to encourage, congratulate, and commiserate.

RSVP within one week to all invitations. Go to an event when you have accepted and call ahead if you can't make it. If you accept an invitation and then fail to attend, call or write to apologize.

Watch your table manners. This can't be stressed enough. Don't stuff food in your mouth or talk while eating. Do not leave your dirty napkin on the table when you excuse yourself during a meal, leave it on your chair instead. Wipe your mouth frequently. When finished, move your fork and knife to the right-hand rim of the plate and sit up straight.

I always treat others the ways I would like to be treated, with kindness and respect.

Becoming a Millionaire

Becoming a millionaire is a more realistic goal than many youngsters—and even many adults —realize. It doesn't takes a stratospheric salary, or a lifetime of self-denial, just a timely and disciplined approach to investing.

It's possible to amass a fortune by saving as little as $50 a month. If at age eighteen you started socking away $50 each month in a stock tax-deferred retirement account that compounds at twelve percent annually, you would amass $755,738 by age sixty—and a whopping $1,377,000 by age sixty-five. Most savings programs are started too late in life to amount to much and many people routinely squander at least $50 a month on items and activities that are essentially frivolous.

God's wealth is circulating in my life.
In everything I do, I always prosper.

Acceptance

Accept the fact that life is not always fair and it never will be. Take responsibility for your life and what happens to you. Take your own action to get your needs met. Ask for what you want.

When life deals unexpected blows, accept them and learn from your circumstances. What is the situation teaching you about yourself? If you blame others, you block learning. You are the master of your own destiny. Have you ever noticed that the experiences you have in life are all very similar, only the faces keep changing or the substances change? You cannot control what will happen in the world. You can, however, control how you will respond.

Always pay attention to your inner guidance. It is always there to guide you on the path best for you. Pay attention and always follow your heart.

I am a stronger and better person because of my challenges. All problems are blessing in disguise.

Look Within

The most growth, the greatest lessons, and the most rewarding transformations occur from the greatest adversities and challenges. Life has a way of making certain past misfortunes pay extra dividends in the future.

You must have the vision to see beyond the appearances of your life. Take time today and everyday to look within and see what your heart is telling you. Practice doing this everyday. If you do, you will soon discover that your happiness comes from within. Awaken to the love that you are.

Carl Jung said: "Your vision will become clear only when you can look into your own heart. Who looks outside, dreams; who looks inside, awakes."

I see all problems as disguised opportunities.
All that my heart desires is coming into my life now.

Putting Play in Your Life

Most adults find it difficult to let go and really play. Work on letting your inner child come out and play and orchestrate your day. Next time you go to the park or even on your jog, do some skipping. If you don't have children of your own, borrow some neighbor kids. Ask them to choose a fun physical activity and let them take the lead. Children can teach us a lot about playing games.

Play hide and seek with adults and children. Walk barefoot on the grass at the park, throw a Frisbee, fly a kite, record a song on a tape recorder and give that tape to someone you love. Use your vacation time to really play. Take along your walking shoes and explore the territory, go snorkeling, or play paddle ball on the beach. Go dancing. Many adults have forgotten how much fun it is to dance. Find a new sport you've always wanted to try and adopt the attitude that this is for fun.

Read a book to a group of children. Better yet, go to a bookstore and buy some children's books for you. Some of them have great messages. One great children's book is *The Velveteen Rabbit* by Margery Williams.

I am laughing my way to health, peace, and happiness.

Dolphins

Dolphins can taste and smell very little; their sense of touch perceived through their thick, smooth skin is more acute. Both young and adult dolphins often play touch games and have extended courtship contacts. They also seem to appreciate being touched by humans. Dolphins use their large eyes well. But it is the dolphin senses of echolocation and sound that allow them to best perceive their world.

Research centers around the world have been gathering data and doing studies with dolphins. From language and cognitive studies on dolphin intelligence, researchers keep learning more about the complexity of their abilities to communicate. In recent years, scientists have made studies about humans with disabilities and dolphins. Much work remains to be done, but initial results seem to show therapeutic effects on both humans and dolphins, as well as enhanced learning performances on the part of the human students.

Like us, dolphins love to play. Fast and tireless swimmers themselves, dolphins enjoy hitching rides. Sometimes they catch the pressure waves made by larger whales, such as the gray. Other times, they ride the exhilarating slipstream formed by a ship's bow or wake. Certain near shore species use ocean waves to body surf just as we humans. The dolphin's well-developed sense of play is one of the many factors that hints at its great intelligence.

Like dolphins, I love to play
at this game of life and live fully.

Junking Junk Mail

Save trees, lighten the load for your mail carrier, and save time from sorting through your mail by having your address taken off the junk mail listing. If you are interested in this, you can write to:

Mail Preference Service
Direct Marketing
P.O. Box 386
New York, NY 10163–3861

I choose to simplify my life
and pay attention to what's really important.

Easing Tension Headaches
with Relaxation

Your imagination may be better than medicine when it comes to treating chronic tension-type headaches. Relaxation techniques like hypnosis, biofeedback, and imagery can sometimes "cure" stubborn, daily headaches when pain medications provide no relief, says Egilius L.H. Spierings, MD, Ph.D., director of the headache section at Brigham and Women's Hospital in Boston.

"People respond much better to treatments that address the underlying mechanisms or causes of headache —tight muscles, for example." That's where relaxation comes in. Dr. Spierings' chronic tension-type headache patients underwent a form of hypnosis, which in one study reduced the number and length of headaches by about thirty percent. Here's how to do it. First, conjure up a vivid picture of your headache in your mind—a big, red balloon filled-to-bursting with water. On the side of the balloon is a tap. Slowly open it, and watch the water drip out, easing the pressure in the balloon. Your pain should subside, Dr. Spierings says.

That technique not only gets you to relax, it also gives you a sense of control. "Many people with chronic headaches suffer from anxiety and depression because they've had this headache for decades and nothing worked," he says. "This treatment seems to empower them." Other relaxation techniques, like biofeedback and imagery, may produce the same results.

I thank the universe for providing me
with opportunities to grow and transform.

Do unto Others

The golden rule of "Do unto others as you would have them do unto you," or "Love thy neighbor as thyself," really makes sense when you understand the importance of self-love and respect. When you are patient and respectful of others, it's because you are first patient and respectful of yourself. And it is only when you forgive yourself that you can practice forgiveness for others.

To create a more peaceful world, choose to live a peaceful life and that starts with tapping into the peace within.

I am lovable, confident, and self-assured.

Prosperity Affirmations

I expect lavish abundance every day in every way in my life and affairs. In everything I do, I prosper. Thank you, God.

I am always in the right place at the right time, abundance is simple and natural to me, all of my needs are constantly met.

God's wealth is circulating in every area of my life. His wealth flows to me easily and effortlessly. All my needs, goals, and desires are met for I am one with God and God is everything.

Miracles are a natural occurrence in my life.

I am constantly giving away the very thing that I desire. I share my wealth with others.

I deserve to be healthy, wealthy, and successful.

God is the source of my supply and all good is mine.

My income always exceeds my expenses.

I invest wisely and responsibility.

I always have plenty of money.

I deserve to prosper.

God is the source of all my supply.

Meditation

Meditation is the natural process of turning within. Anyone can meditate, it just takes disciplined practice. Through regular meditation, you begin to experience the world through new senses. You see beyond your old reality as defined by appearances and enter a state of clarity where inner peace and unconditional love are real and in your heart.

Try meditating twice a day, beginning with twenty minutes a session and increasing slowly as you become more adept. As more people meditate, the effect on the planet will be profound—a more peaceful world will emerge.

God is with me through every change—
guiding, protecting, and directing me all the way.

Thank You

A written or verbal thank you helps people feel appreciated and special. These acts of kindness take so little and can do so much. In a thank you, be specific—mention the time and place when that person did something helpful and that their gesture (a gift, lunch, reference letter) was appreciated. Stay current and, if possible, express your appreciation within forty-eight hours. The note doesn't have to be long nor does the telephone call.

Everyone thrives on feeling appreciated and special. Who can you write or call today to voice your appreciation?

I draw to myself my ideal friends and lovers who share my zest for life and living fully.

Eliminate Bad Habits

Bad habits can be eliminated by replacing them with good habits. Instead of concentrating on what you're not going to do, think about what you are going to do. Instead of thinking that you're not going to eat ice cream, visualize and see yourself eating a healthy diet with emphasis on colorful and tasty fresh fruits and vegetables.

It really helps if you use mental imagery to create a picture of the desired end result. See yourself being healthy and fit and enjoy eating natural, wholesome foods. Remember that it takes about twenty-one days to form most habits, both good and bad. Until that time, you might encounter some resistance in your body and mind in sticking with your agreement. Persevere and you will be successful. For more detailed lessons on releasing bad habits easily and effortlessly, read my books, *Choose to Be Healthy* and *Choose to Live Peacefully.*

I take responsibility for my life
and let go of what no longer serves my highest good.

Get Rid of Clutter

Whether at work or at home, a cluttered environment prevents you from doing your best work. Here are some tips from the book *The Organized Executive* by Stephanie Winston.

There are only four things you can do with a piece of paper: toss it, refer it on to someone else, act on it personally, or file it.

Toss: When in doubt about whether to throw something away, ask yourself: if I should need this document, is it available elsewhere? Or can I capture the kernel of information and then toss the paper? Jot the time and place of a meeting on your calendar, and throw the memo away. Have a drawer to stash uncertain papers that you can check weekly or bimonthly.

Refer: Pass the paper on to someone else who can handle it better than you can. Forward a request for information to someone who has the information. Pass an assignment to a staffer or family member.

Action: Action paper must be personally attended to, like writing a letter of recommendation for a friend who is trying to get into college.

File: The trick to retrieving what you file is to assign your folders broad headings. It's better to have relatively few fat files than lots of thin files. Combine separate files for time management, efficiency, and calendars/planners into a single folder headed "Organization."

I choose to simplify my life and affairs.

Tuning Out Tension

Stress has less to do with your immediate surroundings than with your psychological makeup and your attitude about life. Tension is your body's physiological response to stress. There are ways you can eliminate tension.

Avoid stress-promoting forms of thought and speech. If someone cuts you off in traffic, choose not to be angry. Realize you had no control over the other driver, bless them, and think some positive thoughts instead. Also avoid catastrophic thinking. Don't allow your mind to conjure up all the worst things that could happen in a given situation. When you describe an unpleasant situation, use less severe words and try and focus on the positive side of the situation. What are you learning about yourself? Choose high thinking.

When work or home life gets overwhelming, take a break and replenish yourself. Maybe you only have a few minutes. Closing your eyes and deep breathing will do wonders. If you have an hour or more, go out into nature and pay attention to the beauty around you. Perhaps you might want to read some inspirational book or listen to soothing music. Whatever you decide, take your mind and thoughts off the problem or situation and focus on what makes you calm and relaxed. A change of scenery and activity will leaven and enrich the rest of your day and help to relieve tension.

I am always at the right place at the right time,
radiating the light within me.

Lasting Changes

Major change is not something that happens overnight. The process is similar to learning any skillful act. You need to work with it, practice it, and try to be as consistent in your choices as you can.

Over time these new practices and behaviors become more and more etched into your nervous system as new choices and new behaviors. Sometimes you have to make a commitment to avoid some things for a certain period of time. If you have a problem with alcohol, you probably should not take a job as a bartender. If you are trying to get away from sugar, or trying to change your diet in a certain way, you may want to avoid those things for a certain period of time to give yourself the opportunity to change your behavior and get into your new lifestyle.

Whatever you do for twenty-one days will make or break a habit. So if you want to establish a new habit, either avoid or stick with something for twenty-one consecutive days in a row. After twenty-one days, your body and mind begins to embrace that new habit and no longer craves the old, released habit.

I decide what changes I want to make in my life
and follow through on my commitment.
I welcome change into my life.

Control

Trying to control things or people will cause you frustration and rob you of your peace and serenity. The only things you can really control in life are your thoughts and that is not easy. If you want to enjoy a peaceful, happy life, you must first start with peaceful, happy thoughts and let go of trying to control others.

Do what you can and turn the results over to God. If you surrender your life to God and seek to do His will, then your life will become manageable.

I listen to myself and others
and act confidently with love.

Being Committed

Being committed to your life is the most vital ingredient to living fully and celebrating life. When you completely commit to something, you know it's going to happen and act as if it will happen. The forces within you will move to make it so, and the forces of the universe will also come to your aid.

Faith plus commitment equals manifestation.

I commit myself to take action today
and do those things I know I need to do
to enrich my life and achieve my goals.

Becoming

Can you describe the person you would like to be? How would you look? What would you eat? What career would you have? What leisure activities would you pursue? Visualize this person now. To become this person, act as if you are this person in your current situation. Begin today living your life until you make it a reality.

The more you act as if you are this ideal person, the closer you will be to becoming the ideal person. Your mind will begin thinking like this ideal person. Ralph Waldo Emerson once said, "We become what we think about most of the time." What you believe is what you will most likely achieve. If visualizing or knowing this person is difficult then read about him or her. Select biographies of people similar to your ideal person. Ask someone you aspire to be like if he or she will be a mentor to you and take you under their wing. That will assist in bringing into reality your idealized vision of yourself.

I act as if I am that ideal person I want to become. Every day I am becoming more fully actualized.

Growth with Loss

With all loss in your life comes the opportunity to become stronger and to learn more about yourself. It is often hard to speculate as to the length of time and effort involved in the grieving process but the process is quite valuable. You can choose to succumb to the challenge of loss or work through the pain and grow from the learning experience of release.

Life shows that all relationships are temporary and that separation is inevitable and a natural part of living. Loss comes in many forms: termination of a relationship, completion of a project, job separation, or losing a pet. Loss of conditions is far less tangible, but just as significant. Part of processing loss and learning from it can come in the form of writing, sharing your feelings with others, praying and talking with God, or simply being out in nature.

When you know and feel your oneness with God, you realize that your life is divinely guided and that there is more going on than what you experience with your senses. Through the most challenging changes and loss in your life will come the most rewarding lessons and a profound reverence for life. When you have the feeling that you are being divinely guided, you can move through your loss with grace and gratitude. Your life will be richer and your heart becomes stronger and more sensitive to your purpose. Always be grateful for everything in your life for it's in gratitude that you are most richly rewarded.

I am divinely guided.

Visualize Your Goals

James Allen wrote three quarters of a century ago, "You think in secret and it comes to pass. Environment is but your looking glass."

Your thoughts and visualizations determine your experiences. Each of us has the freedom to accept and embrace whatever thoughts we choose. You possess within the silence of your being the ability to choose your thoughts, to create, and to become whatever you want to become. So take your thoughts off the negative and think only about those things you want to be part of your life.

Every day take five to fifteen minutes and visualize one of your goals. See it in your mind's eye as an already accomplished fact and, in addition to visualizing, feel the emotions of joy and thanksgiving that you would truly feel if this goal were your current reality. And then let go and turn your desired goal over to God accepting that everything you need for your highest good is rushing to you now. Affirm it, believe it, and trust.

I let go of the old and visualize the new.

Choosing to Live Fully

Realize that you can be successful and achieve your goals in life. You carry the seeds of greatness within, that when discovered and nourished, will produce a happier, more rewarding existence for yourself and others.

There is no power greater than your ability to choose. Health is a choice. Happiness is a choice. Living a balanced life is a choice. Radiant health is self-generated. Treatment of disease is something you can obtain in numerous ways from others, but health is something you have to build for yourself.

Sometimes standing for what is good and true and right for you is often a solitary and lonely stand. But this is what marks a true leader — a person who is willing to set an example and to live according to his or her principles regardless of what anyone else thinks or does.

What are you standing for in your life? What are you choosing? Be willing to get out and give it your all.

*I am in constant communication
with my inner creative source.*

Your Body Temple

You are one special being born from the joining of one sperm out of approximately 500 million and one egg. You are already a winner, a divine being comprised of a body, mind, and spirit. You already have everything you need to live your highest potential, to live fully.

It starts with taking care of yourself. Cherish, love, and respect your body temple unconditionally no matter what the current shape. If you'd like to make some changes with your body, make that commitment today to embrace a wellness lifestyle. Choose to eat healthy foods, exercise regularly, think and affirm only positive thoughts about your body and your life, visualize a healthy, radiant body, and live a balanced life.

From this day forward, think of your body in a new light. Realize that it's a magnificent temple and honor the divinity within you. When you live with this awareness, it is much easier to choose to live a wellness lifestyle.

All of my cells are bathed in the perfection of my divine being and are radiating health and vitality.

You Are Magnificent

You are responsible for all your feelings. Never put yourself down. Never think or say anything negative about yourself. Tune into the inner guidance that is with your twenty-four hours a day—that loving guidance that's always there to support and guide you. Dependence on external things happens because knowledge of your own Higher Self, the light within, is ignored. To have this knowledge, you have to practice.

Take a few minutes everyday, a few times a day if possible, and practice loving yourself, tuning into the loving light within and honoring your divinity. Take a walk out in nature and feel your connectedness with everything around you. Breathe deeply. Practice with great reverence.

The universe nurtures and protects me
at all times and in all places.

Changing Your Reality

You have the power and ability to recognize and change the beliefs you have about yourself. Although your beliefs may seem mysterious and complicated on a conscious level, on a subconscious level they may be quite simple. Your beliefs about yourself are based entirely on your past experiences. All of your experiences program your subconscious, and the result is the person you are today.

Start today and only think and speak positively in a way that affirms who you are and what you desire and deserve for yourself. Visualize how you want your life and world to be. You are the master and have the power and ability to live your highest potential. Believe it and live it.

I focus on my highest vision for myself;
my good is rushing to me and claiming me now.

The Fountain of Youth

There is mounting evidence that diseases such as cancer and heart disease are linked to free radicals—substances produced by our bodies in response to normal processes such as oxygen consumption, as well as to pollution, cigarette smoke, X-rays, animal products, and infection. Free radicals can damage DNA and attack healthy cells, setting the stage for many age-related diseases. Certain vitamins and minerals can play the part of antioxidants, neutralizing free radicals and preventing them from harming healthy body tissue, while others help prevent osteoporosis.

The six most beneficial anti-agers are beta-carotene, vitamin C, vitamin D, vitamin E, calcium, and selenium. These anti-aging vitamins and minerals are found in leafy green and cruciferous vegetables, yellow and orange fruits and vegetables, whole grains, nuts, and seeds. If you don't incorporate a healthy range of these foods into your diet, or you eat spartanly to avoid gaining weight, then moderate supplementation of selected nutrients might help. But remember, supplements are an addition to a nutritious diet, not a replacement.

Every day I am getting younger.

Good for You

Sweet Red Pepper: A half cup will give you one and one half times the RDA of vitamin C. The National Cancer Institute recommends at least one daily serving of C-rich food; citrus fruits, kiwi, and cantaloupe will do it, too.

Kidney Beans: They are full of fiber and help lower your cholesterol level. A cup of these beans provides almost sixteen of the twenty to thirty-five daily grams recommended by the National Cancer Institute.

Whole Grain Bread: If it's truly whole grain bread, it's replete with fiber, zinc, copper, magnesium, chromium, and vitamin E. Two nutrient-packed slices comprise up to a third of your needs in the grains group.

Brussels Sprouts: This interesting looking vegetable has an abundance of indoles. This chemical may help to prevent cancer and is also found in others family members like broccoli, cabbage, and cauliflower. The National Cancer Institute recommends several servings of these foods a week.

Apricots: This delicious fruit is a super source of the antioxidants beta-carotene and vitamins. Studies suggest beta-carotene may help protect against lung cancer. Apricots are also full of fiber, and are more nutritious fresh than canned.

I enjoy eating healthy foods
and keep a variety on hand all the time.

Ginkgo Biloba Plus

Ginkgo Biloba Plus is an excellent herbal blend made up of the finest Ginkgo biloba extract, *KYOLIC* Aged Garlic Extract, and Siberian ginseng. It is available at health food stores (see *Resources*).

At a cellular level, Ginkgo protects against structural attack by free radicals, stabilizes membranes, and helps to "tune-up energy production" in the mitochondria of the cell. Ginkgo has been proven effective both against peripheral vascular disorders and disorders of the cerebral circulation. It protects capillaries against becoming fragile or leaking blood into the tissues. Additionally, Ginkgo protects circulating blood against pooling and the formation of clots.

The Siberian ginseng in *GBP* is a standardized blend of the finest Siberian ginseng powder and Siberian ginseng extract powder. *GBP* increases resistance to a wide variety of adverse influences, physical, chemical, and biological in nature, like stress, over exertion, various toxins, and some infections. It possesses a normalizing action on the body.

Combined with *KYOLIC,* the best garlic extract on the market, this herbal blend is an excellent supplement to add to your wellness program to help improve circulation, memory, alertness, concentration, and overall well-being.

Being healthy is my responsibility.
I choose the best for my body temple.

Finally—Truth in Labeling

May 1994 is when the new United States labeling requirements went into effect. The new labeling requires serving sizes to be standardized for each of more than 100 food categories, so that a "low calorie" pie is no longer just a thinner slice. The list of nutrients now includes fat, cholesterol, sodium, protein, and carbohydrates. Under carbohydrate is listed fiber and total dietary sugars. This prevents manufacturers from hiding sugars under other names like dextrose and corn syrup.

I read labels and eat only healthy foods.

Know the Enemy
Sabotaging Weight Loss

It has always been fashionable to blame obesity on excessive intake of carbohydrates, including pasta, bread, corn, rice, and other carbohydrate-rich foods. However, recent research has corroborated earlier findings that the major culprit in excessive weight gain is probably fat. You should not unnecessarily limit carbohydrate intake. These are the foods which give you sustained energy and are actually the lowest calorie source (between fat and protein).

What should be avoided to lose weight, keep it off, and to be healthier is ingestion of fats and oil. Watch out for animal products such as beef, bacon, pork, duck, chicken, sausages, and dairy. Stay away from fried foods, margarine or butter, and foods containing coconut, hydrogenated, and palm oils. Concentrate on fresh fruits and vegetables, whole grains, and legumes, and make sure you get plenty of regular exercise to lose weight and keep weight off.

I choose to let go of anything not for my highest good.

Working Out for You

Who are you working out for? If it's not your-self, then you need to modify your game plan.

Take a good look at your program. (For guidance on developing an individual fitness/weight training program, read *Flawless* by Bob Paris.) See where you can make some changes to help keep you motivated. Add in more variety of activities. Maybe it's just a matter of a few more days off so you have time to recover from an illness or overtraining.

Team up with another person or group of people to help you stay motivated. But the bottom line is that you must workout first and foremost for you. You've got to want to get in shape and be healthier for yourself. No one else will be able to fully understand that feeling of satisfaction that comes after the challenge of a great workout. No one, that is, except you. And that's all that really matters.

Being healthy is a conscious choice I make everyday.

Set Point Theory

Each of us has a biologically predetermined set point for body weight that controls how much we eat and at what rate we burn calories. Dieting and fasting will raise the body's set point. Prolonged or drastic reduction in calorie intake tricks the body into thinking it is starving; the body's natural defense is to slow down the rate at which it burns up food.

A truly permanent weight loss program must involve resetting the set point to a lower level. This can be accomplished by making the following lifestyle changes:

Avoid total daily calories restriction. Less than 1,200 calories a day triggers a starvation response by the body and raises the set point.

Eat smaller but more frequent meals during the day as opposed to one or two larger meals.

Decrease dietary fat to ten to fifteen percent of your total calories.

Avoid refined carbohydrates (sugar), soft drinks, and other fluids containing calories. Excessive sugar releases insulin, which decreases blood sugar, creating the strong urge to eat.

Increase consumption of grains, legumes, and vegetables.

Exercise at least five times a week. Physical activity increases the metabolic rate, builds muscle mass and strength, causes an increased demand for fuel, and adds enzymes that stimulate fat burning.

I now choose to release
any unhealthy food habits and choose life.

Toning Arms, Shoulders, and Chest

Would you like to have stronger and more toned arms, shoulders, and chest? Here's a simple exercise you can do everyday that will make a difference. It's the push-up and you don't need any special equipment. Here's the proper way to do a push-up.

With palms on the floor shoulder-width apart, fingertips slightly turned in and arms straightened, stretch out your body and support your weight with your arms and the balls of your feet. Keeping a slight bend in your waist, slowly bend your arms and lower your body toward the floor until upper arms are parallel to the floor; lift. Do eight to twelve reps.

An easier version: Place your hands on the edge of a low couch or exercise bar.

The easiest version: Same as the first one (top) one except your knees are on the floor, ankles crossed and lifted.

Everyday I find ways to exercise my body
and take loving care of myself.

Self-Esteem and Eating

Food and mood are related in more ways than one. Psychologists at University College in Wales investigated whether people who consumed the most fruits and vegetables would prove to be the best off mentally. That was exactly what they found, but among women only. Researchers discovered that women whose diets were proportionally highest in these foods were the least depressed and anxious.

In earlier similarly well designed studies, researchers found an association between taking vitamin and mineral supplements and better mood, memory, and hand-eye coordination. According to the researchers, these findings suggest that some people are not getting all the nutrients they need. When these inadequacies are corrected with supplements, people feel and perform better.

Because their study showed a food-mood connection in women only they speculate that the powerful female connection between an attractive body and self-esteem leads women who feel best about themselves to eat best, too. A great book to read is *The Love-Powered Diet* by Victoria Moran.

I enjoy choosing foods that nourish my body
and help keep me fit and healthy.

Healthy Role Model

Mothers of daughters who don't exercise should take a look at their own fitness attitudes. Researchers from the University of Missouri at Columbia psychology department held home interviews with 242 fifth- and sixth-graders and their mothers about how much they exercised and how they felt about it.

They discovered that the physically active girls had mothers who were positive that they could stick to their own fitness regimens. These mothers also felt that their families understood and supported their need for exercise. Boys were also influenced by their mothers, but of greater importance to them was participating in sporting events or watching sports on TV. Curiously, whether or not the mothers enjoyed their fitness activities had little bearing on how much the children exercised. For active children, exercise was often a shared family pleasure.

I exercise regularly for myself and enjoy
being a positive role model to other people.

Foods High in Nutrients

Fruits and vegetables are an integral part of any diet that is low in fat and high in fiber, the very diet that health experts think is most likely to help prevent cancer and heart disease. The National Cancer Institute in Bethesda, Maryland, estimates that more than one-third of all cancer deaths are related to diet. And diet high in fat and low in fiber are also considered a significant factor in heart disease.

For more than thirty years, the American Heart Association has been urging people to increase their consumption of fruits and vegetables. A recent study by Harvard Medical School showed a reduced risk for stroke and coronary heart disease among women whose diets were high in beta-carotene and vitamin E, both of which are abundant in vegetables and fruits.

Eating these foods is also a delicious way to obtain nutrients and fiber with almost no fat. By filling up on tender asparagus, broccoli, papaya, strawberries, cantaloupe, or a juicy nectarine, you will be less tempted to reach for a bag of chips. Start today and eat more fresh fruits and vegetables.

I eat only those foods which nourish my body and soul.

The Wonder Vitamin

For years, vitamin C has been hailed as a wonder vitamin. Your body needs vitamin C to aid in healing wounds and absorbing iron—but that's not all. The vitamin, abundant in fruits and vegetables, is one of a group of chemicals known as antioxidants, which researchers now suspect are instrumental in preventing disease. In the process that scientists are still trying to decipher, antioxidants work by neutralizing free radicals, harmful molecules that tamper with the cell's ability to fight disease. A large number of studies also show that a diet rich in vitamin C reduces the risk of cancer.

Some of the best sources of vitamin C include oranges and grapefruit, kiwis, cantaloupe, strawberries, broccoli, sweet peppers (especially sweet red ones), and cauliflower.

My body is a precious gift
and I choose to take loving care of it.

Fruits that Heal

Grapes: All grapes are a great source of boron, a mineral that may help ward off osteoporosis. Red grape juice, made from a juicer, is another healthy pick; besides boron, it contains resveratrol, a chemical that may help prevent heart disease by inhibiting the clumping of blood cells.

Figs: From this delicious fruit, you'll get vitamin C, potassium, magnesium, and lots of fiber, whether fresh found that only fruit fiber, like that found in figs, was linked to reduced systolic blood pressure. All fiber is associated with reduced diastolic blood pressure.

Cantaloupes: Cantaloupes are brimming with beta-carotene and vitamin C, plus fiber, potassium, folate and vitamin B6. Though studies show that betacarotene's anti cancer effect is strongest against lung tumors, it may also protect against oral cancers and cancers of the stomach, cervix, and uterus.

Bananas: This fruit may help lower blood pressure. The magic ingredient? Potassium. Bananas are also rich in vitamin B6, which is essential to maintaining a strong immune system.

*I enjoy the delicious flavors of fresh fruits
and eat them every day.*

The Value of Raw Foods

Much valuable research has been done to clearly show the superiority of raw foods, particularly in the field of enzyme research. These molecules of life force are found in all living plants and animals and are utilized by the human body for every chemical action which takes place in it. In addition to their assistance in digestive processes, they also break down toxic substances, allowing the body to eliminate these without damaging the eliminative organs.

Enzymes are found both within the body and in the food we eat. These food enzymes act only within a very limited temperature ranges and are destroyed by excessive hot or cold temperatures. At approximately 120 degrees F, enzyme destruction begins. As the temperature increases, the tendency is towards further destruction. Cooking processes destroy most, if not all, enzymes. Freezing food is also destructive to enzyme activity.

Choose to eat at least half of your diet raw. See for yourself the difference it can make. *Conscious Eating* by Gabriel Cousens is highly recommended reading.

The foods which promote health and vitality
are the foods I enjoy eating most.

Some Other Reasons
to Become Active

A workout is a personal triumph over laziness and procrastination. It reflects someone who is in charge of their life and takes pride in setting and achieving goals.

A workout makes you better today than you were yesterday. Whether you can feel the difference in your body or not, a workout positively benefits your body and mind. It helps you to see you life from a higher perspective.

A workout is seventy-five percent determination and twenty-five percent perspiration. It's one-part demanded by your body and three-parts demanded by your mind. That translates into one quarter physical exertion, and three-quarters self-discipline.

A workout is a great way to spend your time. You are doing something that will enrich your entire day and leaven the rest of your hours.

A workout is a key that helps unlock the window of opportunity and success. Workouts build confidence and high self-esteem. When you have confidence in yourself, you can achieve anything you desire.

A workout is a form of rebirth. Every time you workout, on some level—whether physically, mentally, emotionally or spiritually—you become healthier and more whole.

Being positive and active is a way of life for me.
I love to exercise.

Healthy Snacking

While a majority of snack foods may be unhealthy, snacking can be very beneficial to your health. Research has proven the efficacy of several small meals each day rather than the usual three large ones. Several small meals increase metabolism and increase body fat loss while sparing lean body tissue. Your body is less stressed and your energy level is more even. Eating several small meals a day will decrease insulin (your body's fat storage hormone) levels twenty-eight percent and cortisol (your body's stress hormone) levels seventeen percent, which translates to a leaner, less stressed, healthier body.

The most natural healthy snacks are fresh, raw fruits, dried fruits (without preservatives), and vegetables. Other good choices include whole grains such as bread products and cereals, and legumes such as black beans or lentils. To keep your energy levels higher and diminish fatigue, your snack should be low fat and high in complex carbohydrates. Studies have shown that a significant source of protein at lunch decreases afternoon fatigue and increases mental alertness.

Most prepackaged foods won't meet these requirements. One exception is PowerBar (only eight percent of its calories are from fat) which has the benefits of fruit, grains (oat bran), complex carbohydrates, vitamins, and twenty percent of the RDA for protein. When you eat a PowerBar, make sure you drink a big glass of water with it to help release all the nutrients.

I joyfully choose foods that align
with my health commitment.

Healing Juices

These juices have helped many people. Of course you should see your physician or health professional for diagnosis and treatment of medical problems.

Alfalfa	Allergies, morning sickness, digestive problems; purifies blood
Apple	Regulates bowels
Apricot	Anemia, constipation, catarrh
Asparagus	Kidney and bladder disorders
Barley	Aid in weight gain
Beet	Builds blood (when combined with blackberry juice)
Beet greens	Constipation; nutrition for liver and gallbladder
Blackberry	Dysentery, diarrhea, anemia; blood builder
Blueberry	Blood purifier
Cabbage	Stomach ulcers
Carrot	Nutrition for eye, hair, nails
Casaba melon	Blood cleanser
Cauliflower	Intestinal cleanser
Celery	Arthritis, neuritis, rheumatism, acidity, high blood pressure, nerves
Chaparral	Arthritis; blood cleaner
Cherry, wild black	Chronic gallbladder trouble (one glass for three successive days, twice a month)
Chive	Catarrhal elimination

Every day I am getting healthier.

Healing Juices II

Cilantro — Strengthens heart, tonic for digestive system

Coconut — Nutrition for bones and teeth

Currant, black — Blood builder

Dandelion greens — Anemia, diabetes, hypoglycemia, low blood pressure, skin troubles

Endive — Aid in weight loss

Fig, black — Laxative

Grapefruit — Aid in weight loss

Grape — Catarrhal conditions; blood purifier, intestinal cleanser

Kale — Hardens teeth and bone

Leek — Catarrhal conditions

Lemon — Aid in weight loss, and for fevers and liver disorders; eliminates catarrhal

Lettuce, head — Sleeplessness

Mango — Irritated intestinal disorders

Mustard greens — Liver and gallbladder cleanser

Okra — Stomach ulcers, irritated intestinal tract

Onion, white — Catarrhal, bronchial, and lung disorder

Orange — Stirs up acids, catarrhal settlements, and hard mucus

Papaya — Stomach and intestinal disorders

I am grateful that nature has provided me with everything I need to be healthy and live fully.

Healing Juices III

Parsley	Diabetes, kidney stones and gallstones; cleanses liver, supports heart, tonic for blood vessels
Peach	Regulates bowels
Pear	Regulates bowels
Persimmon	Irritable intestinal tract
Pineapple	Sore throat, catarrhal conditions; blood builder, aids digestion
Plum (not green)	Laxative
Pomegranate	Bladder complaints
Pumpkin	Body builder
Radish, black	Gallbladder and liver disorders
Radish, red	Catarrh
Raspberry	Anemia; neutralizes acidity
Sage	Digestive and bowel problems, nervousness, night sweats, skin problems, bowel parasites, morning sickness
Squash	Bowel regulator, body builder
Strawberry	Neutralizes acids
Thyme	Headaches, asthma, hay fever, flu, sore throat, eliminates catarrhal from upper respiratory system
Turnip	Body builder; white turnip juice good for asthma, sore throat and bronchial disorders
Watercress	Weight loss

Each morning when I arise
I thank God for my health and this gift of life.

Diet and Medicine

ρ∂ According to a recent Harris poll, Americans are fatter and eat less sensibly that they did in the 1980s. It's no wonder. A study of 3,416 physicians by Cornell University Medical College found that, although over seventy-five percent of physicians realize the importance of diet in disease prevention and the need to improve nutrition training in medical schools, fewer than twenty percent have improved their own diet and very few provide preventive nutrition counseling to their patients.

You have a choice in what doctor you see. Don't go to a doctor who doesn't have a strong background in nutrition and uses that knowledge in his or her practice. Don't look to your doctor to make you healthy. Instead, take responsibility for your own health and adopt a wellness lifestyle. Doctors can lend advice and be available in more serious circumstances but, for the most part, you must take loving and wise care of yourself.

My body is a temple and deserves to be treated with love, respect, and dignity.

Resting Your Body

Health educator Dr. Herbert M. Shelton, who has written numerous books on natural hygiene, emphasizes the importance of resting the body in order to create optimum health. He divides rest into four kinds: *physical rest,* which may be obtained by discontinuing physical activity, going to bed, and relaxing; *sensory rest,* which is secured by quiet and by refraining from using the eyes; *mental rest,* which is secured by poising the mind, meaning ceasing to worry and fret and by the cultivation of mental equilibrium; and *physiological rest,* which may be obtained by reducing physiological activities. This last form of rest may be best obtained by either greatly reducing the amount of food taken or by abstaining from food altogether, as in fasting.

At least once a month, find a day just for yourself. And at least once a week, carve out a couple or more hours where you can rest your body and mind and get away from the world. Your whole life will be the better for it.

I tune into my body and give myself permission to take time off from the world when I need to so I can replenish by body, mind, and spirit.

Vita-Mix Total Nutrition Center

The Vita-Mix Total Nutrition Center is indispensable in my health program. With the Total Nutrition Center (TNC), you can simplify and create nutritious snacks and meals, often within minutes. Rather than filling your pantry with expensive, de-vitalized, packaged foods, you can fill your nutritional needs with whole foods, quickly and easily prepared at the TNC. Discover the flavor of whole food juices, soups, and sorbets that retain the known and unknown phytochemicals and nutrients needed for maximum health. Give your body the staff of life it craves: bread or pancakes made from freshly ground whole wheat. Nourish your cells with delicious salsas that are the freshest possible. And try the 30 other food processes available with the TNC.

For over 70 years, the Vita-Mix Corporation has inspired others to embrace natural, whole foods as a part of a healthier, happier lifestyle with their products. For more information or to order the Total Nutrition Center, see *Resources.*

Each day I wake up feeling energetic and filled
with vitality. I am healthy, happy,
and enthusiastic about life.

Swimmer's Ear

The ear's protective wax barrier has a slight acidity that normally keeps bacteria growth in check. When this delicate acid balance is disturbed, however, bacteria can set up camp. Swimmers, as well as people who frequently soak in water or vigorously swab their ears, are most susceptible to this painful problem. It causes muffled hearing, itchy ears, or sharp pain when you touch your ear or chew.

You can defeat mild swimmer's ear by using a homemade vinegar-and-water mix to banish the bacteria causing your infection. To restore the ear's acid balance, mix a fifty-fifty eardrop solution of white vinegar and lukewarm tap water. Put four drops in your ear three times a day for three days. Otherwise, keep your ear canal dry; use earplugs when swimming and Vaseline-coated cotton balls in each ear before you shower. If you're unsure whether you have swimmer's ear, or if you have an earache, fever, chills, or discharge from your ear, see your physician immediately.

I am grateful for my ears
with which I hear the music of life.

Food Fat Turns to Body Fat

The average American consumes about thirty-seven percent of calories as fat. Research has now found that a diet of ten percent fat of the best for optimum health. With this diet, you can prevent and alleviate heart problems and lose weight easily and effortlessly.

A calorie of fat differs from one of protein or carbohydrate, both in the number of calories per gram and in the way it is metabolized by the body. Protein has 4.3 calories per gram ingested and carbohydrates have 4.0 calories, whereas fat has nine. Your body converts dietary fat calories into body fat with relative ease, expending only three calories to store 100 fat calories as body fat. You would have to expend 23 calories to convert 100 calories of dietary protein or carbohydrate into body fat.

To lose weight and to be healthy, eat a diet high in fiber and complex carbohydrates (whole grains, legumes, vegetables, and fruits) and cut out or way back on animal products, and dairy, oils, and other disease-promoting foods.

Every day I am healthier, fitter,
and more vibrantly alive.

How to Eat More
Fruits and Vegetables

Here are a few ways to include more fruits and vegetables in your diet. At breakfast, drink a glass of freshly made juice or put sliced fruit over your cereal. Eat at a salad bar for lunch but be careful not to load up on fatty dressings. Keep some dried fruit or fresh bananas in your desk.

Buy precut vegetables that can be eaten immediately or prepared quickly. In a pinch, buy frozen vegetables. They are almost as good nutritionally as fresh ones. Add vegetables to your main dish at night, such as adding broccoli to your pasta sauce.

Eat a piece of fruit for a snack when hungry. Have the fruit already washed and ready to eat. Keep a bowl of washed fruit on your dining room or kitchen tables or on the coffee table near the television. If you're hungry before bedtime, eat an apple. Some great books for improving your diet and health are *Food for Life* and *Eat Right, Live Longer* by Neal Barnard, MD, *Fasting and Eating for Health* by Joel Fuhrman MD, and *The Detox Diet* by Elson Haas, MD. Two excellent cookbooks I recommend are *The Health Promoting Cookbook* by Alan Goldhamer, DC and *Everyday Cooking with Dr. Dean Ornish* by Dean Ornish, MD.

*Eating fresh fruits and vegetables every day
makes my body feel fantastic.*

An Unbeatable Combination

Aerobic activity burns fat and helps you lose weight when combined with a low fat, highly nutritious eating program. Aerobic activity is any exercise you can do for thirty minutes within your target heart rate. One of the best forms and most underrated of all aerobic exercises is walking.

Target heart rate means you're getting your heart rate high enough to make you work harder but not so high that your can't carry on a conversation. Your goal should be to work out aerobically—meaning with oxygen. If you're out of breath, ease back so you can talk while exercising.

Keep in mind the following points:

Through aerobic activity, such as swimming, jogging, cycling, rowing, stepping, you burn fuel most efficiently—mainly fat.

You lose weight by aerobic exercise and diet. You tone, firm, and define most efficiently with weight training.

You can't spot reduce. There is no such thing.

Health is not simply about losing weight. It's about being fit.

My body is naturally fit, trim, strong, and energetic.

Relaxation Breathing

Do some diaphragmatic or deep breathing today. Lie flat on your back and place one hand on your abdominal area. If your are breathing diaphragmatically, your hand will rise before your chest. If it does not, focus on inhaling deeply so that your belly expands with each inhalation. This may feel a little awkward initially and may take a couple of weeks of practice for it to become natural. Doing the following three-part breath — inhalation, pause, exhalation — will help you get accustomed to this more efficient way to breathe.

Each part is executed to a count of four to six seconds initially, gradually extending the count to eight or even ten as you become more proficient. Begin by laying comfortably or sitting erect in a chair. Allow all the air to go out of your lungs. Then start inhaling through your nose, deep in your abdomen as you begin to count. Gradually feel the air expand up into your chest, then all the way up to your collarbones. Now hold the count of six to ten.

When you begin to exhale, reverse the order, focusing on each stage as you deflate your lungs. At first practice this twice a day, completing three rounds each time, adding a round as you feel comfortable, up to perhaps twelve each session.

I am grateful for the natural process of breathing which gives me life.

Increasing Your Metabolic Rate

Your metabolic rate is the rate at which your body uses energy at rest. The lower your metabolic rate, the easier it becomes to deposit fat and gain weight. The principal way to increase your metabolic rate, or the body's expenditure of energy, is to increase your activity level. Increasing activity naturally increases energy expenditure. Exercise and increasing the amount of time spent each day walking instead of sitting or riding will help increase your metabolic rate.

One of the best ways to increase the body's metabolic rate is through aerobic or cardiovascular exercise such as brisk walking, jogging, cycling, skating, rowing, hiking, stair climbing, and swimming.

Moderate aerobic activity of any kind consumes up to 400 calories an hour. Aerobic activity also increases metabolic rate for as long a twenty-four hours after the exercise is completed.

Another way to increase metabolic rate and energy expenditure is to increase muscle mass through weight lifting or resistance exercise; muscle tissue is more metabolically active than fat and consumes more calories.

If you are interested in increasing your metabolic rate, then increase your activity through exercise to include at least three twenty to thirty minute sessions of aerobic exercise and two thirty minute sessions of resistance exercise weekly.

My body is in perfect balance and health.

Nutrient-Rich Foods

Sweet Potatoes: These potatoes pack almost twice as much fiber and significantly more beta-carotene than white or red potatoes. In the Harvard Nurses' Health Study, women who took fifteen to twenty milligrams of beta-carotene a day (1/2 cup of mashed sweet potato has one milligram) had a thirty-nine percent lower risk for stroke and a twenty-two percent lower risk for heart attack than women who consumed less than six milligrams of beta-carotene a day.

Pumpkin: This fall favorite is also very high in carotene content, just like its winter squash cousins, butternut and hubbard. All are rich in fiber, too.

Harvard researchers found that women who ate lots of fruits and vegetables high in carotenes—including beta-carotene—had a thirty-nine percent lower risk of cataracts requiring surgery than women who had the lowest carotene intake. Winter squash was one of the strongest protectors.

Spinach: This vegetable is a powerhouse of antioxidants and virtually every nutrient you can think of. It's a particularly rich source of folic acid, which may not only reduce the risk of neural tube birth defects but also protect against cervical dysplasia, a condition that precedes cervical cancer. Another benefit: the ongoing Harvard Nurses' Health Study found that women who ate spinach daily were forty-three percent less likely to suffer a stroke than those who ate spinach once a month or less.

I am grateful for so many delicious healthy foods that I can eat daily.

Exercise for Energy

One of the best ways to increase your energy level is through a regular exercise program. Part of the reason inactivity leads to fatigue has to do with the way we store adrenaline. Activity uses up adrenaline. If it isn't used, adrenaline saps energy and decreases the efficiency of the heart. Thus the downward spiral of energy you feel at the end of the workday will only be worsened if you come home and collapse on your couch or easy chair. Exercise will get the metabolic machinery out of inertia and you'll be refreshed and ready to go.

Start today and make exercise a regular part of your living fully program. It will make you feel great and give you lots of energy.

I am healthy, energetic, peaceful, happy,
and enthusiastic about life.

Celebrate Your Life

Take a moment to close your eyes, breathe deeply, and look closely at all areas of your life. Examine your self-image, relationships, career or business, lifestyle, level of health, income, and peace of mind.

Is your life a celebration, lived as a great adventure? Are you enjoying what each day brings to you, grateful for your life experience, eager to learn, grow, and change?

By virtue of being human, you have the capacity to embrace whatever thoughts you'd like and to become anything you'd like to become. Let go of any thoughts of lack, limitation, fear, and embrace positive thoughts and beliefs about yourself. You have the power and ability to live your highest potential.

Make your life one of celebration, harmony, joy, happiness, success, creativity, and peace. Today find ways to make your life a celebration.

Every day I choose to celebrate this gift of life.

Trusting Yourself

Trust yourself and your soul's inner guidance and you can move through life with grace. Taking responsibility for your life is a joy, a pleasure, and a celebration. Place yourself in charge and become the master of your own life. Since you have control over your own thoughts and actions, you can choose to correct any situation instead of waiting around for someone else to do it for you. This is both empowering and comforting knowing that there is something that can be done about a situation.

Ask yourself, "What can I do for myself here? How could I see things differently?" These kinds of questions are responsible ones, designed to lead you in the direction of true empowerment and trust. Only then can you make the authentic difference that you really want, and move toward the desired state of living fully.

I am grateful for everything going on in my life because it's for my highest good. I have the inner power to create what I desire and deserve.

Choose to Live Peacefully

What would be a greater goal in life than peace of mind? Without it, no amount of wealth or good fortune can ever make you truly happy. With true peace of mind, no adversity or lack can ever disturb your calm center.

Peace and joy are options that you can select at any time. Choose to take wonderful, loving care of yourself, your body temple, and the magnificent world. Live more in the presence of peace and love, which is really living more in the presence of God.

There is nothing in the world more valuable than peace, and it is within you to choose it as a conscious goal. Choose to live peacefully.

When I make God my highest priority,
all other priorities fall into place.

You'll See It When You Believe It

Visualization is an amazing process to help you achieve your goals and dreams. Earl Nightingale's "strangest secret" was "You become what you think about." And William James said, "You think in secret and it comes to pass. Environment is but your looking glass."

Everything in your life had its beginnings with your thoughts and what you imagined. If you want to make some changes, start by changing those images and what you expect. The people who are successful in life are those who continually think about the people they would like to be and the lives they would like to live.

Your subconscious doesn't know the difference between fantasy and reality. When you continually focus on all the positive things you'd like to have or how you want to be, your subconscious will accept that as a command and use its marvelous powers to bring your dreams and aspirations into reality. The key is to consistently visualize yourself exactly the way you want to be, regardless of appearances. And in addition to seeing your dreams in your mind's eye, equally important is to feel those emotions of joy and thanksgiving you would feel if your vision were your reality now. "Act as if" you were living your vision in everything you do.

I see myself living my highest potential
in every area of my life.

Take a Word Inventory

The words you think and speak have a tremendous influence on your life. You literally live the words that are a permanent part of your thinking and speaking patterns. For example, have you ever said something like, "he's a pain in the neck," or "that's back-breaking work," or "she drives me crazy?"

These seemingly harmless expressions can program garbage into your subconscious. The subconscious mind does not know that you don't really mean those things. It just plays them out into your life, into your experience, as if that's what you really want.

Watch what you say and only affirm those things you want to bring into your life and your world. Your words are very powerful. Choose them wisely.

Every word I speak reflects the presence of love
in my heart and soul.

Henry David Thoreau

Henry David Thoreau truly lived a simple life, always paying attention to his inner guidance, not interested in what other people thought of him. "Do what you ought to do," he wrote in his journal in 1854. "Why should we ever go abroad, even across the way, to ask a neighbor's advice? There is a nearer neighbor within us incessantly telling us how we should behave. But we wait for the neighbor without to tell us of some false, easier way."

Thoreau did not believe in the ordinary values of society. "Most men, even in this comparatively free country, through mere ignorance and mistake, are so occupied with the factitious care and superfluously coarse labors of life that its finer fruits cannot be plucked. Their fingers from excessive toil, are too clumsy and tremble too much for that. Actually, the laboring man has not leisure for a true integrity day by day.... He has no time to be anything but a machine."

He was genuinely shocked to find people spending so much of their lives making a living and so little in fulfilling the higher purpose for which he believed man was created.

Are you living fully, fulfilling a higher purpose? Are there things you can change in your life right away to help you live more fully?

My higher purpose is clear to me
and is fulfilled because I live with the awareness
of my oneness with God.

Sharpen Your Mind

Would you like to sharpen your memory? Try exercising. A study conducted at Utah State University found that working out sharpens memory. The study partitioned volunteers into three groups—one that did water aerobics three times weekly for nine weeks, a control group that went on with their lives as usual, and a third group that socialized together, going to plays, basketball games, and slide shows. Unlike those in the social or control group, the people in the exercise group significantly increased their short-term memory, particularly verbal recall which helps with names, directions, and phone numbers.

My memory is sharp and active
and I keep it that way with a healthy lifestyle.

Tips for Snorers

You can always slip into another room, yet maybe some of these tips will help alleviate the snoring.

Try sleeping with your heads at opposite ends of the bed. Putting a little distance between your snoring and your partner's head will decrease the loudness.

Get some soft ear plugs, the kind that shape to your ear.

If you are overweight, lose weight. Only ten pounds of extra weight (increased fat) can affect the airway and add to the volume of snoring.

See that you get adequate amounts of sleep. When a snorer is more tired, the throat muscles become more limp, blocking the airway, which causes more snoring.

Don't drink alcohol for at least two hours before going to bed. It causes muscle relaxation.

Be aware of medication. Sedatives, even allergy pills, may increase snoring by causing throat muscles to relax. Ask your doctor about dosages.

Have some white noise in the background, such as a tape player that plays the sound of waves or a waterfall.

Visualize no longer snoring.

My sleep is relaxing and peaceful.

Buying a New Car

When buying a car, make sure you know what the car is worth. You can't negotiate on equal terms with a car salesman unless you know the value of the car. Your local library should have a number of sources listing the precise amount the dealer paid for the car you want to purchase. Add to this cost the accessories you have chosen, taxes, plate fees, and about one and a half percent for advertising. Present this total to your salesperson and if they come back with a counteroffer of $200 to $500 over your calculated cost, take the deal. But if they refuse your offer, don't walk away. Instead, ask to see the boss. Many times a salesperson won't cut such a close deal because it'll cost them a chunk of their commission, but the dealer will.

Timing is also important. In the past, all new cars came out in September. So if you wanted a good deal on a close-out, your best bet would be to go shopping in late August or early September, just before the new models arrived. Now car dealers introduce new models throughout the year. To get the best buy on a close-out, ask the dealer when the next year's line is due out.

Pay attention to the rebate. Manufacturer's rebates come directly from the manufacturer and not the dealer. So when buying a car, don't let the dealer figure in the rebate while you're wheeling and dealing. Contact the manufacturer directly for up-to-date rebate information.

In all my business dealings,
I act with integrity and inner guidance.

Winning an Argument

In *The Power of Ethical Persuasion* by Tom Rusk, MD is some good advice if you find yourself in an argument.

Listen up. The single most important thing you can do to win an argument is to let the other person present their entire point of view without any interruptions.

See it their way. After your opponent finishes presenting their case, restate their view before you present your case. "People are more likely to be swayed by your logic if they feel you understand them," says Dr. Rusk.

Don't get personal. If you're arguing over a business deal, don't bring up his bad golf swing to prove his lack of judgment. It'll only make him mad and less willing to concede.

In my dealings with other people, I keep in mind that we all want to be appreciated, respected, and loved for who we are and not simply for what we do.

Protecting Your Heart

More than a million and a half Americans will suffer heart attacks this year. Half a million of them will die, most before they reach the hospital. Diet can help prevent heart disease as well as speed your recovery from a heart attack. Here are some guidelines to keep you on the right track.

Eat the equivalent of one cup of cooked beans, peas, lentils, or oatmeal everyday.

Don't skip meals.

Eliminate or at least reduce your meat, poultry, or fish intake to three ounces, three times a week.

Avoid butter, margarine, cheese, and egg yolks. If you eat dairy, only nonfat sources.

Pick nonfat foods first; low fat foods in a pinch.

Have two to four servings of fruit per day.

When hungry for seconds or a snack, make vegetables your first choice.

Choose sodium-free or low sodium products.

Use only nonfat and low fat cooking techniques like grilling, broiling, baking, steaming, or poaching. Sauté with water, lemon, and garlic instead of oil.

Use vegetable oils sparingly and first choose mono-unsaturated oils, like olive and canola. Spectrum Naturals (see *Resources*) makes excellent oils; they are available at your local health food store.

I look upon my day with a smiling heart.

Negotiating

Do you want a raise, your children to go to bed on time, a nicer office, or a parking spot in a crowded garage? Then you need to know how to negotiate to get what you want. Successful negotiation will hinge on one major factor: preparation. Being prepared means knowing not only what *you* want but also being able to explain to your supervisors what's in it for them. Here are some other important do's and don'ts by Nicole Schapiro, author of *Negotiating for Your Life.*

Don't go in cold. Bring in some facts that you've prepared in advance.

Don't pitch to the wrong person. See the decision maker.

Don't force your style on someone by giving reams of paper to a bottom liner, or one piece of paper to someone who only acts on reams of information. Do be aware of your employer's or other person's personality and work style; try to match it.

Don't become overly emotional. Do stay calm and focused on your goal.

Don't assume anything. Know what you know and what you don't.

Don't argue or attack. Do be willing to make concessions without forfeiting your goal.

Don't start out too low. Do start high. If you want a $5,000 raise, ask for $8,000. When you get $5,000, both you and your employer will feel like winners.

I am financially self-sufficient and happy in my work.

Stop Stomach-Sleeping

Sleeping on your stomach twists your neck, compresses blood vessels and nerves in your arms, and hyper extends your lower back. It also increases the lines on your face. You'll need three to four pillows and about three months time to wean yourself from it.

Step One: For the first four to six weeks, lie on one side and stack two pillows in front of your chest, another under your head and at least one between your knees to keep you from rolling over.

Step Two: For the next four to six weeks, sleep with a pillow under your head and one to two between your knees. (The farther apart your knees are, the less likely you are to belly flop.)

Step Three: Try sleeping one night a week without the pillow(s) between your knees. Gradually increase the number of nights you sleep without the pillows. If you wake up on your stomach, replace the knee pillow for a night.

I rest in the faith, love, and peace of God.

Food for Thought

Peace of mind is not circumstance dependent. I love you because that's my nature. I like you because I choose to.

What you are is God's gift to you. What you are becoming is your gift to God.

Pain happens whether we like it or not but there's a certain kind of suffering that's optional. Pain is mandatory in life; suffering is optional.

We always have a choice in any situation to see the love or fear. In all situations and at every moment, choose your highest thought.

Living in the presence of God is recognizing God's indwelling presence, which is always love, life, and power within us. It is now ready and waiting to flow forth abundantly, lavishly into your consciousness and through you to others, the moment you open yourself to it and trustfully expect it.

God made us one with Him. When you recognize this fact, claim your birthright, and live from that awareness, the Divine in you will be manifested in your life and world.

The divine Presence within is your sufficiency in all things, and will materialize itself in whatever you need or desire. Expect it. Live with an attitude of gratitude.

Every experience in life has the potential to bring me closer to God.

Making a Commitment

Without commitment, life would not be as rewarding and fulfilling. It's not until you make a commitment to something, and follow through on your commitment, that you'll see the fruits of your dreams and desires.

If you are ready for commitment, you will make your words count and not lose momentum with obstacles and challenges. When committed, you immediately arrange your personal circumstances so that your lifestyle totally supports your commitment. You will do the things you need to do to order your life, eliminate non-essentials, and focus on what is important. Add faith to your commitment, and the world is yours for the asking.

Faith plus commitment equals manifestation.

I am continually aligned with my higher purpose.

Tips for Safer Driving

Clean the other side of the glass. It's not enough to clean the outside of the windshield. You need to clean the inside regularly, too. You always have a certain amount of film collecting on the inside of the windshield glass that reduces visibility, particularly at dusk and at night and makes headlight glare worse.

Let tailgaters pass you. What do you do when someone tailgates you? It's best to just let them go by. You're better off being safe than right.

Drive with your headlights on all the time, even in daylight. With headlights on, you're visible at a distance of about 4,700 feet and without headlights, only about 2,200 feet. You don't have to wait for failing light or bad weather to drive with your headlights on.

Don't rely on your mirrors before you make a lane change. Blind spots are always there. So before you make any lane change, take a quick look over your right or left shoulder.

Also: Check your tire pressure and tread frequently; replace worn tires as soon as possible. Always keep an eye on your headlights and taillights to make sure they are operating properly. Carry emergency first aid equipment in your trunk; include a space blanket and a flashlight with fresh batteries, especially for winter weather.

I am always divinely guided and protected.

Love as a Healer

Love is a powerful source of healing in your life and choosing to love is a key to healing yourself, your relationships, and your world. If you want to live in a peaceful and loving world, you must first live as a peaceful and loving person. As you learn more about who you are, a divine child of God, you will discover that love is a universal power available to everyone. Healing can occur when you open your heart and join with other people to share dreams, disappointments, hopes, and fears. When you are willing to ask for help in giving and receiving love, help is given.

Healing calls for replacing fear with love. This begins with practicing forgiveness. Forgiving yourself as well as others opens you to love. Learn to be discerning rather than judgmental and recognize that mistakes are for correction, not for condemnation. When you are not afraid to make mistakes, you can learn to love yourself and others more fully.

Young children are masters at forgiving, loving, and living without judgment. In return, they are so lovable. Be more childlike in your approach to love and life. Everything a child touches is new, special, and filled with joy. Life becomes a celebration of love.

Find ways to love today. Love everyone in your life. Find pleasure in loving. To love is to find pleasure in the happiness of the person loved.

I see God's light in everyone I meet
and celebrate this oneness in us all.

Parenting

As early as possible, let kids do things for themselves—even if they are slow and not yet skillful. Letting children handle life's early demands and get a little scared helps them develop skills they will use later.

Empathy does not mean agreement. It means understanding how your child feels from his or her point of view. Accept that the emotions are real for the child; whether or not you agree with them is unimportant. This helps children feel understood, essential for a healthy sense of self.

Don't take sides when kids fight or ask who started the fight as that will only make things worse. Don't make weak statements about not wanting them to fight. And don't berate them for fighting; they are just good people who are behaving badly.

If you happen to be arguing with someone else in front of your children, explain to them that even people who love each other sometimes have differences of opinion, because they are different people. Make it clear that having an argument does not mean you don't love each other. It's important to help children see that it is normal to express anger. Children who never see their parents angry may feel guilty about their own angry feelings.

Just as adults need private time in their lives regularly, so do children. Give them private time, even when they are very young. This will help them understand that adults need some time alone, too. It will also cultivate their inner peace and serenity.

I express my feelings with honesty and inner guidance.

Being a Good Listener

Here are some of the ways you can be a better listener.

Offer nonverbal cues to show you are paying attention. You can nod, smile, lean forward, or put your hand on someone's shoulder. Facial expressions can mirror the tone of what the other person is saying—smile when the speaker laughs, frown slightly when he or she frowns. Small verbal phrases of encouragement can also build empathy.

Finally, look at the speaker when they're talking. Look directly in their eyes. Don't let your attention wander off to check out everything going on around you. Give that person your undivided attention and let them know by your gestures and support that you care.

I listen to what others say with my ears and my heart.

A Healing Attitude

A positive attitude can be a potent weapon against serious illness. In one group of leukemia patients, twelve of thirteen who were characterized as being highly depressed died within a year of receiving a bone marrow transplant, but thirty-four of eighty-seven patients who were not depressed were still alive after two years.

In a study of men who had heart attacks, twenty-one of the twenty-five most pessimistic died within eight years, but of the most optimistic, only six out of twenty-five died.

A human being can change his or her life just by changing his or her attitude. Adopt a positive attitude today no matter what appearances are telling you. As within, so without.

I am a healthy, happy, radiant, and positive person.

Secrets of Savings

It's hard to save money and hold on to your income. In 1948, the median income American family paid two percent of its income in taxes to the federal government. In 1992, that same family paid twenty-four percent of its income to the federal government and as much as nine percent in state and local income taxes. Here are a few ways families and individuals can hold onto more of their income.

Have a clear picture of your cash-spending and your cash-earning potential. Sit down with your checkbook or your bank statements and checks for the past couple of months. On a piece of paper, draw a vertical line down the middle of the page. List your income for the month on one side and your spending on the other. Add to your monthly spending a portion of the big outlays, such as house payments and car or medical insurance, that you might pay once or in a few installments. When you get to the bottom of the page, the totals will tell your story.

Are you spending more each month than you earn? Are you financing the difference with debt? If so, it's time to take action. Are there ways you can supplement your income? Finding ways to earn a second income can be a lot less painful and more fun than many of the alternatives, such as cutting way back on spending.

If you can earn extra money, perhaps by doing something at home, don't spend the extra money you're earning. Use it to pay off debts.

I am doing what I love and feel passion for
and am getting paid generously for it.

Loneliness versus Aloneness

There are many positive qualities to being alone and finding peace in your own company. Find ways in your life to be in solitude daily, weekly, and monthly by carving it into your schedule. In being alone, you find time for introspection, reflection, growth, and inner development. The mentally healthy person needs time alone as well as time with others.

It not uncommon to push yourself to be with another person simply to escape loneliness. See loneliness as a healing period that allows you to tread a new path by choice, not out of a need to escape. From loneliness comes aloneness and then the joy of solitude. Make friends with aloneness today and everyday. It will leaven the rest of your hours and make your days and life much brighter.

I live in the peace of my own company.

Anger

Anger is never beyond your control. You are always in charge of your own thoughts and reactions to everything that happens in your life.

One of the primary ways to deal with anger is captured in this ancient quote by Epicetus: "If you do not wish to be prone to anger, do not feed the habit; give it nothing which may tend to its increase. At first, keep quiet and count the days when you were not angry: 'I used to be angry every day, then every other day; next, every two, then every three days!' and if you succeed in passing thirty days, sacrifice to the gods in thanksgiving."

I'd rather be happy than right.

Dealing with Anger

Anger must be expressed in appropriate ways. Often anger will be resistant to leaving unless you acknowledge it. A brief expression of the feeling by yourself, or with a trusted friend or therapist, can unlatch it from its powerful position. Center your mind on all the good in your everyday life—on any evidence of beauty, love, or harmony. No matter how inconsequential the item may seem, if the power of thought is behind it, it has the potential of creating a better reality for you. It might be the smell of a flower, the view of a sunset, or the loving expression of a friend or family member.

Let go of expectations and judgments. This will take you a long way in preventing and releasing your anger. Realize that "this too shall pass" and it probably won't make any difference a month or year from now. Most importantly, put your life in God's hands and remember that everything that happens carries with it the potential for growth and positive benefits.

Today choose to let go and let God knowing that everything that happens has the potential for good. If you feel anger, acknowledge and express it appropriately and know that your life is in divine order.

Rather than seek pleasure and avoid pain and anger,
I accept both as having equal benefit.

The Comfort Zone

The comfort zone is the area in life of familiar people, places, things, and activities. If you are not expanding your comfort zone and embracing the new, then this zone is shrinking and trapping you inside. To live fully, have the courage to face the fear of breaking out of this comfort zone.

Face your fears and expand your comfort zone. When you feel resistance to action or new ideas, pay attention. Look at the resistance carefully. Is it fear only? Then face your fear and go against the resistance. Expanding your comfort zone will keep you growing in body, mind, and spirit.

I face my fears and expand my comfort zone whenever I have the opportunity.

Positive Thinking and Arthritis Pain

Relaxation training, more adaptive coping skills, and family support may reduce aching and swelling in people with the chronic pain of rheumatoid arthritis. Researchers at the University of California at San Diego divided fifty-nine men and women, ages twenty-five to seventy-five, into four groups. One group attended ninety-minute "behavioral treatment" sessions with a family member once a week for six weeks. During the sessions, the group practiced progressive muscle relaxation and deep breathing exercises. They also learned to change negative self-talk to more positive thoughts, like "This will end; I can cope." Another group received the same treatment without the family member present. The third group attended videotaped presentations about rheumatoid arthritis, with a family member and discussed the tapes afterward. A control group received no treatment.

The behavioral treatment groups reported actual physical changes in their joints and less pain and depression than the education and control groups after the six-week period. Significantly more patients in the behavioral groups experienced a fifty percent reduction in joint pain than patients in the other two groups. In addition, they had less swelling and fewer painful joints. There was a slight reduction in the number of pain medications used by patients in both behavioral groups. Most of those improvements were still evident when researchers followed up again two months later.

Every moment of my life is filled
with the love and peace of God.

Successful People

Daniel Isenberg at the Harvard Business School studied twenty-five of the most successful executives in the country to find out what they did to make them successful. For one week, he followed each person, listened to phone conversations, listened to them talk to their friends and family, and came to the conclusion that what made these people successful had nothing to do with what they teach you at the Harvard Business School. There are two important qualities these successful people had in common.

The first thing they all had in common was spiritual sensibility. Some of them were church goers, some were not, but they all had this sense that there was this deeper intelligence in the universe that operated through their heart and an incredible faith in their intuition. They all made their decisions based on their intuitive feelings about what was going on with their businesses or professional corporations.

The other thing successful achievers had in common was putting their values first. When goals came in conflict with values, values were taken care of first.

Are you in conflict with what you want to do right now and what you feel is the right thing to do? Pay attention to your intuition.

I am attuned to divine inspiration.

Be Loving and Kind

Love and kindness are expressed in countless, caring ways whether loving yourself or loving others. One very effective way to be loving and kind is by hugging.

Being hugged causes your body to release endorphins. Known as nature's uppers, these are the chemicals your body releases when you feel great. Endorphins increase your resistance to disease and help diminish pain. There is a great deal of healing that occurs when you touch another human being.

Look for opportunities to hug others. If by chance you're spending the day alone, then take advantage of this special time to give yourself several hugs during the day. Never underestimate the power of hugging. Even if the other person doesn't seem to outwardly receive value from your hug, know that your hug is benefiting their body and soul.

As I feel self-love, I experience the love of others.

Living with Awareness

Ninety-five percent of us accept things as they are and five percent will do things differently. When you live with awareness of your oneness with God, you know your power and use it to create what you want and to find ways to serve others. Life is about giving your love away and about celebrating life.

It doesn't matter where you are or what you are doing. The key to experiencing a heightened state of awareness is to focus your attention on love, on God. Mental disciplines like meditation are invaluable, because they help concentrate your attention and enable you to climb the inner summits of your mind. As your mind becomes free and clear you can experience everything in your life from a higher perspective. It's almost as though you have grown new eyes, new ears, and a new heart. Let your heart be filled with the love of God today.

With a thankful and grateful heart,
I keep my awareness on love and peace.

Creating What You Want

If there are things in your life you would like to change, you have the power within to take charge and make the desired changes. It all begins with your thoughts and what you envision.

The subconscious part of your brain doesn't reason, it is merely programmed. When you integrate this knowledge into your life, you will be able to create a healthier, happier life than ever before.

The subconscious works to create reality according the programming it has been fed. Although this is normally accomplished by thoughts and through your life experiences, brain researchers have found that the subconscious is incapable of telling the difference between reality and fantasy, between the real experience and the imagined experience. Visualize the desired changes you want. See with your mind's eye the end result of something you want such as a healthier body, a more loving, nurturing relationship, a more prosperous and satisfying job. Along with visualizing, feel inside you those feelings of joy and thanksgiving that you would feel if this vision were your current reality. Do this for a few minutes everyday and you'll see your life changing for the better.

Everything I need to know is revealed to me.

Vitamins of the Air

The air we breathe contains a large number of good and bad compounds. Some of these are essential nutrients in the form of vitamins, minerals, and trace elements. Air is much like food—there is "junk" air and "good" air to breathe. Bad air makes the mind and body feel terrible, while good air, like good food, awakens the senses and enlivens the being. Junk air is full of positive ions while good air is charged with many negative ions.

Nature provides us with an abundance of negative ions near waterfalls, by the ocean, in the mountains, and after a good thunderstorm. However, indoor environments like our offices, cars, and homes, are all but devoid of valuable breathable nutrients. Restoring the negative ions to your environment can be a key to making you feel better, look younger, and live longer.

When a high quality air ionizer, capable of delivering millions of extremely small, ingestable negative ions is placed beside the bed on a night stand or on a desk, a large invisible cloud of negative ions forms which the individual breathes in and starts feeling better. When used regularly, negative ion therapy can help restore vitality, promote better health, and enhance the individual's physical and mental well-being by providing the vital air nutrients that are as essential to us as food nutrients. For information about air ionizers, see Bionic Products in the *Resources*.

*Every day I take time out to slowly inhale
and exhale to revitalize my body.*

Nutrition Flash

According to the new federal label law, "low fat" indicates that no more than thirty percent of the product's calories come from fat. To watch your fat intake, check labels that say the food has no more than three grams of fat for every one hundred calories. Many nutrition experts feel that this is still too high. Make sure you don't get more than one to two grams of fat for every one hundred calories.

The ten best grains are quinoa, amaranth, buckwheat groats, bulgur, barley, wild rice, millet, brown rice, triticale (a cross between wheat and rye), and wheat berries (or uncracked bulgur). These were ranked tops nutritionally (in that order) by the Center for Science in the Public Interest. Yet most people tend to eat less healthful wheat, oats, corn, and white rice. It's time to diversify.

If you take a beta-carotene supplement, make sure you take it with a meal, since any fat you eat will help your body absorb the antioxidant. You'll get up to triple the benefit if you split the same amount among three meals. There is essentially no absorption after fasting. Better yet, eat three carrots a day.

Raw foods every day help keep the doctor away.
I always keep fresh fruits and vegetables on hand.

Eat Dinner at Lunch Time

The French eat their main meal at lunch, and they suffer fewer heart attacks than Americans, even though they ingest the same amount of fat. Researchers comparing the eating patterns of fifty Parisians and fifty Bostonians noted that the French consumed fifty-seven percent of their calories by 2 P.M. The Americans, who ate their large meal after work, had taken in only thirty-eight percent of their calories by that time. The researchers speculate that when you eat the bulk of your calories earlier, your body is better able to metabolize the fat. As a result, blood cells called platelets are less likely to aggregate—or stick together—which reduces the incidence of clotting that can lead to strokes and heart attacks.

Take a week and experiment with eating lightly at dinnertime three hours before going to sleep. You'll feel a difference and have more energy.

*My body is healing and rejuvenating itself
moment-to-moment.*

Some Healthy Tips

People who adopt a low fat diet suffer fewer day-to-day feelings of depression and anger. Cutting down on fat will also reduce your risk of heart disease and obesity, too. Cutting down on fat is one of the single most important diet changes you can make in your life, along with eating lots of fresh fruits and vegetables daily.

If you can't have just one, don't drink at all. One drink is defined as twelve ounces of beer, five ounces of wine, or one to one and a half ounces of hard liquor. Women's smaller bodies have less water than men's to dilute alcohol, and only half the amount of alcohol dehydrogenase, which breaks alcohol down in the stomach before it reaches the bloodstream and from there the body tissues. Excess alcohol that the body can't comfortably process in this way puts a strain on the liver. If you want to experience radiant health, don't drink at all.

Stop dieting and break the yo-yo cycle. The latest evidence indicates that a lifetime of repeated gaining and losing of that "last" ten to twenty pounds contributes to heart disease, not to mention low self-esteem.

I embrace the practices which make me healthier
and bring me closer to God.

Superiority of KYOLIC
Aged Garlic Extract

For more than 5,000 years, garlic has been known as a preserver and restorer of health. There are many garlic supplements available on the market and none of them compare to *KYOLIC*. The manufacturing process, comparative studies, and clinical studies guarantee the superiority of *KYOLIC* Aged Garlic Extract over other garlic products (see *Resources*).

Only the finest quality raw garlic is used to prepare *KYOLIC*. The quality of the garlic, organically grown on Wakanaga's farm, is examined to ensure that it meets rigid specifications. The unique, natural aging process which takes twenty months increases the effectiveness of garlic and eliminates side effects such as odor.

KYOLIC has been scientifically studied all over the world and been found to prevent fatigue, heart disease, cancer, and immune disorders. It has been found to possess anti-oxidant properties, lower levels of serum cholesterol and triglycerides, improve appetite in children, lower blood pressure and have a salutary effect on arthritis, insomnia, hemorrhoids, allergies, and the common cold.

I live in harmony with nature
and provide my body with only the best of everything.

Fats and Oils

Today health scientists understand a lot more about the relationship between the kinds of fats and oils consumed and health and longevity. Some studies suggest that the manufactured saturated fats (also known as hydrogenated fats) are potentially the most harmful to health. These fats contain trans-fatty acids, a type of fatty acid that rarely occurs naturally but is produced in the manufacturing process through hydrogenation. Trans fats produced through hydrogenation are synthetic saturated fats mutated from polyunsaturated or monosaturated oils. Hydrogenated fats are common ingredients in processed foods and margarines.

Current studies suggest that an ideal diet might provide about fifteen percent of calories from monounsaturated fats (in the form of canola or olive oils) and five percent from supplements oils (like Spectrum Naturals Veg Omega-3 Flax Seed Oil and Wheat Germ Oil).

Oils become rancid after prolonged contact with air, light, and/or heat. You can identify a rancid unrefined oil by its unusually strong unpleasant odor and sharp or bitter flavor. To protect your unopened oils from spoilage, store them in a cool, dry place, out of harsh light. Keep the opened oils you use daily in the refrigerator. Freezing is a good way to extend shelf-life, especially with the super-reactive supplement oils (flax seed or wheat germ oils) sold in plastic containers.

To assure top quality, use oil made by Spectrum Naturals (see *Resources*).

Divine ideas are new possibilities
that I welcome and act on.

Happy Teeth

Starch, not sugar, is your teeth's worst enemy. Sweets can cause cavities, but foods like potato chips and crackers are actually more likely to linger in the teeth for hours. Brush as soon as possible after eating both sugary and starchy items. You'll be helping to keep your teeth in good working order for later years.

My smile is the shortest distance between myself and others.

Ways to Live Longer

One of the easiest ways to add years to your life is to eat all kinds of fruits and vegetables and lots of them throughout the day. New research shows that leafy, crunchy fruits and vegetables may play a more crucial role in longevity than has ever been suspected. The National Cancer Institute recommends five daily servings of this food group, which is the key source for many top cancer-fighting nutrients and other substances such as fiber, beta-carotene, vitamin C, and vitamin E. Recent studies reveal that the last three may also help prevent heart disease, cataracts, and other age-related illnesses.

Once every seven to ten days, take a day or two and eat only fresh, raw fruits and vegetables. In only two days, you will see a positive difference in your skin and have a feeling of lightness and radiance. Doing this every once in awhile also helps to break bad food habits. Give it a try and see what a difference it can make in your life.

I celebrate this gift of life
and greet each day with joy and enthusiasm.

Cutting Boards

Wooden cutting boards are more sanitary than plastic ones for cutting up raw poultry and meat. Researchers at the University of Wisconsin contaminated a variety of boards with salmonella and other bacteria. Within minutes, bacteria on the wood disappeared (perhaps trapped by wood cells) or died; old boards eliminated germs most effectively of all.

Conversely, bacteria thrived on plastic and were not easy to wash off, particularly if the surface was scratched. Don't forget, whatever type you use when cutting meats and poultry, make sure to wash the knives, your hands, and anything else that touches the food very thoroughly.

I face life's challenges with enthusiasm.

A Little Exercise Goes a Long Way

Attempting to burn 1,000 or more calories a week through exercise if you've been sedentary all your life is indeed difficult, despite the lure of such benefits as the lower risk of heart disease, diabetes, and many other ailments. However, your heart can benefit from far less exercise than that to be aerobically fit — exercise that significantly increases your heart rate for twenty minutes, three times a week in order to increase your body's ability to use oxygen.

Less exercise can still offer much benefit, an attractive prospect for the elderly who are not so physically capable. Walking three miles a day, five days a week, for twenty-four weeks, increases levels of HDL, the "good" cholesterol that protects your heart. Not surprisingly, the faster walkers achieved greater aerobic fitness.

Middle-aged women at or near menopause who exercise the equivalent of walking two miles, three times a week maintain constant levels of HDL, whether or not they also lose weight. The decline in HDL cholesterol after menopause may be one factor responsible for the subsequent rise in heart attacks in women.

I choose to be with friends
who are positive and enthusiastic about life.

Sprouts

The kings of live foods are sprouts. Fresh sprouts are truly alive, still in the growth process when consumed, the product of a germinating seed. Practically any whole bean, grain or seed, unless chemically treated, can be sprouted. Besides the popular bean and alfalfa sprouts, lentils, garbanzo, buckwheat, sunflower seeds, mung beans, soybeans, amaranth, triticale, rye and wheat berries can also be sprouted.

Once beans, grains, or seeds are sprouted, the carbohydrates and the calories are reduced, the vitamin B content increases, vitamin C, which is absent in the dried bean, is generated, and if sprouts are exposed briefly to sunlight, chlorophyll and vitamin A appear as well.

You can find sprouts ready to eat in most produce sections and you can sprout your own at home. Sprouts are a very important part of any nutrition program; eat sprouts several times each week. For more information on sprouts, read *The Sprout Garden* by Mark M. Braunstein.

I am sprouting with enthusiasm and vitality.
I have a zest for life and living fully.

Creating a Fit Body

Eat Breakfast. Your body burns calories at a slower rate as you sleep. Breakfast is your metabolism's wake-up call, kicking it into calorie-burning mode. If you don't eat something in the morning, you may ultimately burn fewer calories. Choose fresh fruit for breakfast.

Build Muscle. To lose more fat, you have to build more muscle. Even when you're sleeping, your muscles use up twenty-five percent of the energy you burn, and the more muscles you have, the more energy you burn. With bigger muscles, you burn more calories, no matter what you're doing: running, walking, mowing the lawn, reading the paper, even sleeping. The best way to build muscle is by weight training.

Go Out and Graze. Eating small meals throughout the day—instead of two or three large meals—may be better for fat burning. After you eat, your body releases the hormone insulin. The larger the meal and the higher it is in fat and sugar, the more insulin your body releases in response. Insulin causes your body to save fat and make fat from carbohydrates. It even helps turn your fat cells into magnets for the dietary fat floating around in your blood stream. But smaller meals eaten more frequently keep insulin levels lower and more stable.

Grazing, of course, only works if you choose the right foods: high complex carbohydrate, non-fat foods like baked potatoes, whole grains, beans, and vegetables.

All the cells in my body
are radiating health and vitality.

Firming Your Chest

Here's a simple exercise to firm and tone your chest muscles (pecs) that can be done at home or at the gym. Holding some weights (or two soup cans or laundry detergent bottles), lie with the small of your back pressed firmly into a bench, knees bent, feet flat on the bench. Extend your arms out to your sides at shoulder level, elbows rounded, palms facing each other. Lift both arms toward each other above your chest until the weights touch. Bend your elbows and lower the weights until your hands are on either side of your chest. Press the weights back up over your chest, then lower your arms out to starting position.

For an easier version: Use lighter weights if needed.

The easiest version: Do this exercise on the floor instead of a bench with lighter weights.

My body is toned, fit and perfectly shaped.
I love to workout and I do so each and every day.

A Taste of Fat

Despite the surge of new low fat products, sticking with a low fat diet doesn't seem to be getting any easier. Frequent tastes of fat, even in low and fake fat foods, perpetuate the desire for it. But one can learn not to like that creamy taste so much.

This type of learning is called a "hedonic shift" away from fat, and researchers have found how to reeducate one's palate in about twelve weeks. Three groups were used; one served as a control, and two groups were put on low fat diets with fifteen to twenty percent of their calories coming from fat. One of them used special low fat versions of fatty foods; the other ate no modified foods. Those who were allowed the special low fat foods were able to get frequent tastes of fat throughout the day without exceeding their fat allowance. They were not denied the sensory pleasure, the "mouth feel," of fat.

In twelve weeks, the taste preferences of those who were not allowed modified foods had changed. They rated the high fat test foods as less pleasant.

Because my health is important to me,
I choose foods that are low in fat
and emphasize lots of fresh fruits and vegetables.

Super Foods

Barley: Contains beta glucans, a type of soluble fiber that can lower your risk of heart disease. Hull-less, waxy varieties (found in health food stores) contain the most beta glucans, but any barley is a good source. Look for the term unpearled on the box; this means the barley is unprocessed and higher in fiber.

Carrots: These bright orange vegetables are best known for their sky-high beta-carotene content. Eating one carrot a day may reduce the risk of lung cancer among ex-smokers. Eat at least one carrot each day or make some fresh carrot juice.

Cabbage: This is an important member of the cruciferous family of cancer-fighting vegetables. Its anti-cancer key may be the presence of substances called indoles. Scientists think that one indole in particular may help prevent breast cancer by decreasing the activity of the chemical estradiol, which is a precursor to the hormone estrogen (estrogen fuels the growth of certain tumors).

Brown Rice: It contains a substance called oryzanol, which reduces LDL levels by as much as twenty percent. (The high fiber rice bran found in brown rice may help lower cholesterol, too). Brown rice shines in vitamin B6 and magnesium, while also providing thiamin (important for the functioning of nerves), niacin, copper and zinc. And it also has vitamin E which strengthens the immune system and reduces the risk of heart disease and cataracts.

Day by day, I am becoming healthier and more joyful.

Getting Better Faster

Uncooperative patients get better faster. To a doctor, uncooperative means asking many questions, being persistent, researching your illness, and examining your own medical records. Patients who are more knowledgeable about their condition and participate in the decision-making process receive more satisfactory care from their physicians.

Take charge of your health and body. Research, ask questions, and find out everything you can on how to be healthy, to heal your body, and to create a glorious life.

*I am responsible for my health
and am in charge of my own life.*

Activity and Your Heart

Active people tend to have healthier hearts. Walking, running, cycling, and swimming all raise your good (HDL) cholesterol levels, keep you trimmer, and make your heart more efficient so it doesn't have to work as hard to pump the blood where it's needed.

Accumulate sixty minutes of activity each day. At least thirty of that sixty should be blocked out for one uninterrupted aerobic session. The remaining active minutes should come from other activities such as gardening, carrying groceries, walking up or down stairs, playing tennis, mowing the lawn, or mopping the floor.

What's good about this program? It gives you more than the bare minimum of thirty minutes, three times a week, usually recommended, and it gives you credit for every physical activity you do, so achieving the hour isn't so difficult. And since it's more than the bare minimum, missing occasional days is no disaster.

My healthy, active lifestyle brings me great joy
and an appreciation for life.

Think Chromium and Calcium

Fresh fruits and vegetables as well as whole grains all contain small amounts of the trace mineral chromium. People who don't get enough chromium can't use their insulin as efficiently to get sugar out of the bloodstream and into the body tissues. This could be an early warning sign of diabetes. Ample chromium also helps to keep extra weight off and develop lean muscle tissue. Sugar drains the chromium from your body.

Calcium is important to grow strong bones. Milk and other dairy products are not the only sources of calcium. Cows get their calcium from grasses and dark green leafy vegetables. The following foods have high amounts of calcium: kale, carrot, collard green, Swiss chard, broccoli, sesame seed, and quinoa (grain).

Each day I love to eat a variety of health-providing fruits, vegetables, and whole grains.

Cooked versus Raw Foods

Live foods are surrounded by a considerably stronger bioluminescent field than cooked foods. This field is associated with greater cell bioelectricity and life force. Cooking also destroys the zeta potential in food, which means it destructures the biological fluids in the food and consequently in your body. This results in poorer nutrient transfer in the cells and clumping of the red blood cells as well as other imbalances in the energetic system of the body.

If you eat cooked foods over a long period of time, this depletes the enzyme reserve of the body. Enzyme reserve seems to be connected to life force, health, and longevity. Enzymes, which are a type of protein, are living biochemical factors that activate and carry out all the biological processes in the body such as digestion, nerve impulses, detoxification process, functioning of RNA/DNA, repair and healing of the body, and even the functioning of the mind. The preservation of your enzymes by eating live foods plays an important role in slowing the aging process.

Don't underestimate the importance of raw foods in your diet. For excellent reading on raw foods, get *Spiritual Nutrition and the Rainbow Diet* by Gabriel Cousens.

I love myself and want to take special care of my body.
Raw foods are part of my daily health program.

Honeybee Pollen

No ordinary food is good enough for the honeybee. It needs incredible amounts of energy to fly on the average of 15 miles per hour and between as many as 1200 flowers in one flight from the hive. Honeybees collect and eat pollen grains from flowers—one of the wonder foods of nature—as they pollinate the flowers at the same time.

According to scientists, bee pollen is a highly concentrated source of essential elements which seem to be the most complete food in nature. Studies reveal bee pollen's ability to increase the body's resistance to stress and disease and speed up the healing process in most conditions of ill health. It also possess age-retarding and rejuvenative properties. If a nutritionist were to take all the available research and knowledge to develop the perfect all-round dietary supplement, he or she would come up with one not far removed from honeybee pollen.

The honeybee products I take and recommend come from Premier One Products. Their wide variety of products are far superior to any bee products I've ever seen (see *Resources*).

I am a powerful and healthy person.

Fruits and Vegetables

Give your diet a disease-beating boost by eating the recommended five to nine servings of fruits and vegetables daily. It's really not as hard as you think.

One serving equals one medium-size piece of fruit or one half cup sliced; three quarters cup juice; one half cup chopped raw or cooked veggies; or one cup leafy greens. If you're not currently eating much produce, build up your intake gradually to allow your digestive system time to adjust.

Aim to eat two fruits or vegetables at each meal, plus one or two every day as snacks. Try to eat fruits alone and not combine them with other foods. When you eat fruits this way, they go through your system efficiently and quickly, providing you with immediate energy and nutrients.

I love taking good care of myself
and being an example of radiant health.

The Weight Game

Liposuction is not the only solution to a cellulite problem. Liposuction is very dangerous and the results are not always beneficial.

Cellulite is nothing more than body fat. Cosmetic firms and spas have given it this special name to promote their special treatments. The fat cells we call cellulite are identical to the fat cells everywhere else on the body although they take on a different appearance in certain areas. Women tend to have a larger concentration of fat cells in the hips and thighs. This is called the gynoid pattern of fat deposition. Men have a larger concentration of fat cells in the abdominal region. This is called the android pattern of fat deposition. An excess amount of fat storage in either area will yield a dimpled appearance.

When you lose weight by dieting without exercise, much of the weight lost will be lean tissue (muscle). This means that although you might be at your ideal body weight, you may still have a high percentage of body fat, at least higher than what is recommended. Diets by themselves don't work. You must exercise regularly with aerobic exercise (brisk walking, cycling, jogging) in addition to doing some weight training to increase your lean muscle mass.

My body is toned and lean.
I eat healthy foods and exercise regularly.

The Weight Game II

The recommended percentage of body fat for women is fifteen to twenty-five percent. For men it's between ten to twenty percent. Have your body fat measured at least two times each year so you can evaluate your training and adjust it and your nutrition program as needed.

How low the percentage of body fat must be to lose the cellulite is different for everyone. But be assured, the only way to lose it is to burn it off through aerobic exercise, when muscle uses fat as fuel, and to do some weight training to increase your lean body mass and to tone and reshape your body. Also cut the fat in your diet down to no more than fifteen percent of your daily calories.

Cellulite cannot be sweat, vibrated, massaged, or rubbed away. Low fat nutrition and regular exercise will cause your lean percentage (bone and muscle) to increase while your fat percentage decreases. As this shift takes place, you may even experience an increase in total body weight, but this is good because this increase will be in bone and muscle, not fat. Don't use the scale every day. You may even want to throw it away or, at least, not use it more than once a week. You will be able to tell how you're doing by how your clothes fit and how you look in the mirror better than what your scale says. Forget liposuction, change your diet, and get into the habit of exercising regularly. It's an unbeatable combination for losing fat or cellulite and creating the body you've always wanted.

When I look in the mirror,
I choose to see all my positive qualities.

Slanting

Gravity is the master of your environment. From the moment you enter this world your life is dominated by this universal force. You can avoid unhealthy foods, contaminated water, and polluted air, but you cannot get away from gravity. Gravity can have a negative effect on posture, skin tone, circulation, concentration, and all of the organs of the body as it relentlessly pulls them down. Gravity never lets up.

Learn to work with the law of gravity instead of allowing it to work against you. Try lying on a slant board, which puts the legs higher than the heart and the head lower than the heart. In this position, the pull of gravity on your face, neck, back, organs, legs, and feet is naturally and effectively reversed.

Use of the slant board reduces or eliminates headaches, insomnia, varicose veins, chronic fatigue, and neck and shoulder tension. It can improve posture, complexion, and circulation and foster relaxation and peace of mind. The BodySlant and Body Lift (see *Resources*) are highly recommended. Always check with your doctor before slanting, especially if you have high blood pressure.

The laws of the universe are always supporting me
in being the best I can be.

Greater Health Foods Tips

Stay away from fried foods or any heated oils. Those foods clog your arteries and make you fat.

Thoroughly chew your food. Chewing well increases the efficiency of digestion. Eat slowly. If you are in a hurry, skip the meal or have some fresh fruit.

Don't eat until you are hungry. It's better to wait until you have a keen desire for the plainest food.

If not entirely comfortable in mind and body, do not eat. Food is not digested well when you are upset or uncomfortable.

Do not eat beyond your needs. Most people eat more food than their bodies need and that puts extra stress on your body. There have been countless studies done around the world showing that the healthiest and longest living people do not overeat.

Give thanks for your God-given, health providing foods. Eat simply to live.

I eat to live, not live to eat.
Nature has blessed me with delicious foods.

Flax Seed

Flax seed may be one of nature's greatest little health packages. With an abundance of Omega-3 and Omega-6, two essential fatty acids, plus fiber (both soluble and insoluble) and lignins, you get an excellent package to help rejuvenate your system.

Essential fatty acids are the basic building blocks of every cell in the body. Unfortunately they are processed out of food through hydrogenation, which preserves the food. The essential fatty acids have also been shown to help in reducing harmful triglycerides in our systems that cause hardening of the arteries and other related problems. With a multitude of vitamins and minerals in flax seed, it's a superlative food to prevent degenerative diseases and promote radiant health.

Fiber is very useful in the fight against cholesterol in our bodies and it keeps the intestinal tract and colon cleansed. The lignins found in the fiber of flax are converted within the body to lignans. High levels of lignans in the bowel have been associated with reduced rates of colon and breast cancer. Flax fiber provides about 800 milligrams of lignan precursors per gram, compared to only eight milligrams per gram in common fiber such as bran.

For the best flax seed powder on the market, look for Fortified Flax (see *Resources*) at your health food store.

My mind and body are healed
through the power of love within me.

A Touch of Health

Therapeutic massage is a traditional, age-old healing practice that has experienced a great resurgence in popularity in the last quarter century. But until recently the therapeutic benefits of massage have largely been relegated to intuition and ancient wisdom. The University of Miami's School of Medicine has opened "the first institution in the world for basic and applied research on the sense of touch," the Touch Research Institute (TRI). Their projects have included research into effect of massage on immune function with AIDS and cancer patients, touch and addictions, and the effects of touch on physical and emotional development.

There are some impressive initial results: premature "crack babies" given three fifteen minute massages each day for ten days suffered fewer medical complications, an astounding twenty-eight percent greater daily weight gain, and displayed more mature motor behavior by the end of the ten-day period. With regular massage, abused children living in a shelter became more sociable and active. Massage made preschoolers more focused, and adult office workers more alert. HIV positive males who received five massages a week for a month showed improved immune function and significantly reduced anxiety and stress.

If massage sounds interesting to you, consider taking classes in your area from an accredited masseuse and get a massage table for your home or office.

The essence of my being is love and radiance.
I honor my marvelous body by taking care of myself.

Making the Most of Fruit

Fruit is one of the healthiest, most cleansing foods you can eat, especially when you eat fruit on an empty stomach. Two to four servings of fruits a day can help prevent cancer, heart disease, and a list of other ailments. It's important to have a variety of fruits in your diet.

When juicing fruit, make sure that you drink it immediately as much of the nutritional value is lost if you let it sit around, even for a few minutes. Eat as wide a variety of fruit as possible for a full range of nutritional benefits. A fruit salad of papayas, melons, and raspberries can be a nutritional cornucopia. Mix fresh fruit juice with sparkling water for a delicious and nutritious spritzer. Or try combining one or two pieces of fruit in a blender with some fresh fruit juice and a frozen banana for an especially refreshing and healthful smoothie.

Everyday I find ways to get fresh fruit in my diet.
I am radiantly healthy and filled with a joy for life.

Mind-Body Connection

Mind-body medicine is based on treating the total patient. Hippocrates defined health as the harmonious balance of mind, body, and environment. What's new about mind-body medicine in the 1990s is the growing body of scientific evidence that verifies the value of ancient healing traditions. Dean Ornish, MD, has revolutionized heart therapy by demonstrating that chronic heart disease can be reversed by lifestyle changes alone, without the use of drugs or surgery. Ornish's patients adhered to a very low fat diet, quit smoking, exercised, and followed a stress-reduction program that included yoga, meditation, and group support. After one year, eighty-two percent had more blood flow to the heart and clearer arteries. Results after four years on the program were even more dramatic.

Heart disease is the number one killer in the United States, and the annual cost of angioplasties, bypass surgery and other treatments amounts to a whopping $87.1 billion (according to the American Heart Association). The implications of Ornish's findings appear truly significant.

My health is a result of thinking healthy thoughts and living a balanced life—physically, mentally, emotionally, and spiritually.

Reshaping Your Body

If you are interested in losing weight or reshaping your body, include exercise in your program. Combined with a healthy, low fat nutrition program (not diet), exercise will speed up the rate you lose weight, and will help to give you the fit, toned body you desire and deserve.

Exercise combined with eating a low fat, nutritious diet helps guarantee that you lose mostly body fat, not lean muscle tissue. Exercise increases muscle mass, which in turn increases metabolism and burns calories. After exercising, individuals have a higher metabolic rate for as long as fifteen hours. Exercise, especially weight training, builds muscle tissue which sculpts, shapes, lifts, and defines your physique.

Exercise helps reduce inches. Instead of weighing yourself, measure yourself. The tape will show you how the size of your hips, thighs, and waist are changing (so will the mirror and your clothes).

Aerobics and strength training are the best exercises for your weight loss regime. Aerobics speed up the breakdown of fat and tones your muscles, and strength training builds and develops sleek, strong muscles. Muscles will never turn to fat—they are entirely different substances and one cannot become the other, so don't be afraid to build beautiful muscles. Cycling, walking, jogging, swimming, skating, rowing, and stepping are the most popular forms of aerobics.

*My precious, miraculous body shines
with health and vitality.*

Lessons in Truth

In her book *Lessons in Truth*, H. Emilie Cady offers practical and spiritual guidance to create a life of love, peace, prosperity, joy, happiness, and creativity. Her focus is on living from the awareness that you are a child of God and already have everything you need to live your highest potential.

She writes, "No matter how sick or weak or inefficient you seem to be, take your eyes and thoughts right off the seeming, and turn them within to the central fountain there, and say calmly, quietly, but with steadfast assurance: *This appearance of weakness is false; God, manifest as life, wisdom, and power is now flowing into my entire being and out through me to the external.*"

Whatever you want is already in this surrounding invisible substance; faith is the power that can bring it out into actuality. Spend time each day sitting alone in meditation and silence with your mind continually in an attitude of waiting upon God. Jesus had many hours alone in communion with God. But Jesus didn't spend all His time in receiving. He poured forth His knowledge of spiritual things to constantly uplift and to help others. His life was about service and that's where you will find true happiness.

Luck is meditation and preparation meeting opportunity. You are a very lucky person when you live in partnership with God.

I speak the words of thanksgiving for this gift of life.
I greet each day with a thankful and cheerful heart.

Cycling Is on a Roll

The most energy-efficient form of human transportation is the bicycle. It can transport you around town for errands or to work and back with the least energy expenditure of any mode of transportation. Why commute to work and back, and then try to find the extra time to burn your extra calories? You can save gas, parking, and other transportation costs, and even time by commuting to work by bicycle. Klein (see *Resources*) manufactures quality road, hybrid (good for the mountains and the road), and mountain bikes for people whose main mode of transportation is cycling.

Many companies across the country are now encouraging their employees to cycle to work. Fleetwood Enterprises, Inc. of Riverside, California has gone so far as to purchase bicycles to loan to their employees for a three-month trial period, after which they can be bought by the rider at a substantial discount. Ride your bike to work for three or more days a week, and the company provides helmet, reflective vest, mirror, and a light — free! Get a flat tire and someone from the company will come out and pick you up. Maybe your company will consider something similar.

In a recent survey, twenty percent of commuting motorists revealed that they would cycle to work if there were more bike paths. Where can you fit cycling into your life?

I enthusiastically pedal through my days
which brightens my life in so many ways.

Looking Upward

Sri Ramakrishna was a spiritual leader whose goal was union with God. He used to tell this parable, or allegory, on how prophets attained their wisdom and peace.

"There is a fabled species of birds called homa, which live so high up in the heavens and so dearly love those regions, they never condescend to come down to earth. Even their eggs, which when laid in the sky begin to fall down to the earth, attracted by gravity, are said to get hatched in the middle of their downward course and give birth to the young ones. The fledglings at once find out they are falling down and immediately change their course and begin to fly upward toward their home, drawn thither by instinct. Men such as the great prophets are like those birds; even in their boyhood, they give up all attachments to the things of this world and betake themselves to the highest regions of true knowledge and divine light.

"As an aquatic bird, such as the pelican, dives into water but the water does not wet its plumage, so the emancipated soul lives in the world but the world does not affect him."

I am interested in the higher spiritual things of life.

Live the Life You Imagine

Henry David Thoreau once said that the world is but a canvas to our imagination. If you don't like the way your life is going, change your thoughts and visions and focus on those positive things you want to create in your life. Thoreau sums it up best in the end of *Walden:*

"If one advances confidently in the direction of his dreams, and endeavors to live the life which he has imagined, he will meet with a success unexpected in common hours. He will put some things behind, will pass an invisible boundary; new, universal, and more liberal laws will begin to establish themselves around and within him; or the old laws will be expanded, and interpreted in his favor in a more liberal sense and he will live with the license of a higher order of beings. In proportion as he simplifies his life, the laws of the universe will appear less complex, and solitude will not be solitude, nor poverty, nor weakness. If you have built castles in the air your work need not be lost; that is where they should be. Now put the foundations under them."

By visualizing daily how you want to live and be, you will rapidly move forward to accomplish your goals and aspirations.

*I am healthy, wealthy, happy, and peaceful
because I see myself being this way.*

Self-Reliance

Self-reliance comes from inner knowledge that you are connected to a higher power that is always there to guide your every step and answer all your questions. Perhaps one of the greatest examples of self-reliance is Henry David Thoreau.

An original thinker, Thoreau offered a solution in simplified living and self-reliance, the deliberate reduction of one's wants to a level that could be easily satisfied, and still leave time to cultivate the garden of the soul. In *Walden* he writes, "A man is rich in proportion to the number of things he can afford to let alone. My greatest skill has been to want but little."

Find ways to simplify and to pay attention to what's really important in your life.

I am rich indeed because I am connected to God and all my needs are constantly met.

Let's Meditate

Prayer is talking to God and meditation is listening to God. Meditation begins with stilling one's thoughts and emotions and calming your mind and body. Like everything new, practice regularly to get good at mediation. When you first begin, your mind will probably be flooded with thoughts. Instead of trying not to let thoughts and emotions enter your mind, dwell on positive, opposite practices that will exert a calming influence on your mind. The breath is an excellent way to calm your mind and body. When you're ready to meditate, sit up with a straight spine and do a few deep breathing exercises. Breathe in while counting to four or six, and then breathe out to the same count. The more you do this, the longer you'll be able to count.

As you are deep breathing, concentrate on relaxing more and more deeply—not just physically, but mentally and emotionally. Feel every part of your body relaxing and becoming lighter. With your eyes closed, look upward, concentrating your attention at the central point between the eyebrows, the seat of spiritual vision. Offer up all thoughts and feelings in deep concentration at this point. Perhaps you'd like to mentally say to God, "Reveal Thyself, Reveal Thyself." Gradually, and with practice, you will begin to feel the divine peace permeating your body and mind and you will know that your are safe and protected and that there is this peace beyond all fear.

God is with me through every change—guiding, protecting and directing me all the way.

Listening to Children

Take your children's feelings seriously. Don't minimize their concerns. Acknowledge those feelings and say, "I can see that this might be scary for you." Then, follow up with an encouraging comment, showing them that you have confidence in their ability.

You also shouldn't assume your children are worry-free just because they haven't told you that they are anxious. Often, it's hard or embarrassing for kids to articulate what they're afraid of.

Instead of waiting for your children to bring up the subject, do so yourself. If you can help your youngsters find the words to talk about their fears, you'll be better able to address their questions and concerns as well as let them know you're available to listen.

I always pay attention to my inner child and create an environment of safety and acknowledgment.

Teaching Your Dog

If you have a dog, or know someone who does, these tips may come in handy when teaching the dog new tricks.

Keep lessons short. Four quarter-hour lessons will be more productive than one full hour.

Give lessons at the same time and place each day, in an area where there are no distractions.

Don't attempt to teach just after the dog has eaten a full meal.

Keep lessons consistent and interesting.

Make sure you've got the dog's attention before giving a command.

Limit commands to one or two words. Use the same tone of voice all the time.

Praise or criticize the dog during an act, not afterward, so it knows what it has done right or wrong.

Wait until the dog learns one lesson before moving on.

Command with firmness and authority, yet with kindness and patience. Do not show displeasure if the dog makes a mistake — stop if you find yourself losing patience.

Always finish with a game.

I give love and respect to all animals.

Popular Alternatives

Alternatives to regular medical care are becoming increasingly popular. In a recent survey of over 1,500 adults, more than one in three said they had used unconventional therapy in the past year, like chiropractic, massage, relaxation therapy, spiritual healing, and other practices not used in hospitals or taught in medical school.

The alternative therapy was often in addition to medical treatment, with more than eighty percent of those who used unconventional therapy for serious medical problems also seeing medical doctors for treatment. But most of these patients didn't tell the MD about their alternative treatments — even though knowing this information could be important.

Be open to all kinds of treatment and, most especially, pay attention to your inner guidance which is always available to assist you on the right path.

*I always talk to God and listen to my inner guidance
before making decisions.*

Are You Left-Handed?

Not long ago, there was a study revealing that lefties die sooner than right-handed people. The major source of confusion was there were so few lefties over eighty years old because many years ago many natural lefties were pressured to become right-handed.

If you have young children who are beginning to use the left hand predominantly over the right, don't force them to change. Let their natural instincts guide them on what's good for them.

*I am constantly attuned to my uniqueness
and to the voice of divinity within me.*

Facials

A professional facial can make a man, woman, or teenager feel refreshed and pampered, but some may actually be harmful to the skin. There are no federal requirements in the United States regarding cosmetologists, so each state licenses them individually. Only ten states have a separate license for skin care. In the other forty states, a licensed hair dresser can legally perform facials. Regardless, there is no guarantee that the person performing the facial will be a professional, so consider checking the following areas before make an appointment:

Check out the salon. Be sure that they have a license for the salon itself and another for the individual cosmetologist. Get a reference from a friend.

Note the general appearance and hygiene of the salon; if less than spotless, look elsewhere.

Make sure the facialist's or cosmetologist's nails are cut short to minimize risks of damaging the skin.

For those with cystic acne or any chronic skin condition, a facial has potential for irritating the skin and make the condition worse.

Watch for signs that a facial is being performed too vigorously. An overactive facial is one that hurts.

Wait for at least a few hours after the facial before applying makeup (if you can wait overnight, it's even better).

Beware of mild chemical peels offered by some salons. These can cause problems in some people and should only be done by licensed physicians.

I take care of my body temple and treat it with respect.

Appreciate Life Today

Night by Elie Weisel describes his experiences as a holocaust survivor. As a child, Weisel had to sleep with corpses and not know from day to day if he was going to survive. He said it was like he was living a nightmare. The first night he was there, he saw children being thrown into the flames alive. Early on, they went through a line sending some people to the left and some to the right. Everyone in his family was ordered to go to the right while Weisel went to the left. He found out later that everyone in the right line was killed.

Even though six million people died in these concentration camps, never give up on humanity. Have faith in every human being and live with love in your heart. In spite of all Weisel went through, he loves life and wants everyone to do the same.

Remember the holocaust and never let it happen again. Live with peace in your heart and extend the peace and love within you to everyone you meet in life. That's what you're here to do. Learn to be more peaceful, extend it to others, and connect to the love within.

I expect a miracle to occur at any moment.

Reducing Stress in Your Life

Whether you are young or older, work in an office or at home, have children or not, are educated or school or by life itself, there are difficulties and challenges in daily life which create stress. But there are ways of looking differently at these circumstances so they don't become overwhelming.

Always remind yourself you are able to cope even if the worst does happen. You have much more resilience than you realize. Don't think of all the bad things that can happen. In almost all cases, the worst never happens anyway. Don't worry about what other people think and say. Concentrate on fixing the problem.

Make a decision and set up a course of action to come up with a solution for your difficulty. Don't make your problem more serious than it really is.

Always consult your intuition or inner guidance. All the answers you need to anything in your life can be found within you if you just ask for guidance, be patient, and act on what you receive. In any problem or challenge, any situation or circumstance in life, love is the answer.

I trust myself and my intuition.

Antidote to the Blues

Exercise can shield you from the blues. How exercise works so effectively is very complex. Some suggest it distracts people from their problems; others say it increases recall of pleasant memories. And a majority of research claim that there are chemicals released in the body as a result of exercise which lift spirits and make you feel happier and more positive.

An added bonus is that exercise helps to dissipate anger. Keep exercise always on the top of your list of activities to be radiantly healthy—physically, mentally, emotionally, and spiritually.

I give thanks and praise for all things
and exercise my choice to be happy.

Beat the Heat

It's a muggy day or just very hot — a good time to watch out for heat exhaustion. No one is immune to heat exhaustion, not even the best-trained athlete. The cause of heat exhaustion is dehydration and loss of electrolytes; the hotter it gets, the more you sweat. Sweat is nature's cooling system. But if you sweat too much, you run low on water, and your cooling system shuts down. Thirst is likely to be the first symptom of oncoming heat exhaustion, followed by loss of appetite, headache, dizziness, and even nausea. To avoid it:

Drink water. It is still the best way to rehydrate. But sip, don't gulp. Better yet, drink plenty of water before going out in the sun or heat.

Eat lots of fruits and vegetables. They have plenty of water as well as a good electrolyte balance.

Avoid salt tablets. Increased salt in the stomach keeps fluids there longer, which means there's less fluid for sweating and cooling off the body.

Avoid alcohol and caffeine. Both of them speed dehydration. Dousing your head and neck with cold water will help prevent heat exhaustion.

Wear a hat. Your head and neck gain and lose heat very rapidly, but a wide-brimmed hat with lots of tiny holes will keep your head cool and ventilated.

*Under the most challenging circumstances,
I remain cool, confident, and at peace.*

Flax Seed Oil

Essential fatty acids (EFAs) are nutrients the body can't synthesize; these must be supplied by the diet. The two EFAs are Omega-3 (alpha-linolenic acid) and Omega-6 (linoleic acid). The glands need EFAs to carry out the secretion of hormones and other regulating substances. In the muscles, EFAs help the cells to recover from use and overuse.

The contemporary Western diet is lacking in Omega-3 and over-supplied with Omega-6. According to Udo Erasmus, author of *Fats and Oils,* North Americans consume about twenty-five percent of the quantity of Omega-3 needed for optimal health. Fish oils have Omega-3 but research shows that fish oils also contain traces of pesticides and industrial pollutants such as PCBs and mercury.

Flax seed oil contains a concentrated source of Omega-3 fatty acids which is also rich in natural tocopherols, compounds that act as an antioxidant in the body to protect other molecules and cell components.

Spectrum Naturals (see *Resources*) is known for the nutritional quality of their flax seed oil. Their top quality Veg Omega-3 Organic Flax Seed Oil is made from organic flax seeds, and their unique oil removal process eliminates the damaging consequences of light, air, and heat.

Veg Omega-3 Organic Flax Seed Oil is available at health food stores. Include it in your health program.

I express love and appreciation
for my marvelous and miraculous body.

Your Child's Teachers

Visit your child's teachers. Parents who take the time to do this really stand out and so do their children. Teachers, like other people, respond best to attention and appreciation. They perform better for children whose parents are appreciative of their hard work and are interested in their children's development, not just their grades.

My inner child is healthy, happy,
and celebrating this gift of life today and always.

Sleep

New and exciting findings in sleep research have helped many stay healthier, both physically and emotionally, and work better. Most adults need seven-and-a-half to eight hours of restful sleep to function well and teenagers do better with ten hours. One-fifth of the United States population complains of the inability to fall asleep or to stay asleep.

The costs of sleep deprivation are irritability, falling asleep at work, wavering attention, and not fully processing the outside world. Tension, physical or psychological, keeps us from relaxing sufficiently to fall asleep. People are literally taking their worries to bed. Learn techniques for coping with stress and "winding down" before bed. Relaxation techniques such as deep breathing, stretching, and meditation are very helpful. Regular exercise is also a terrific way to help you sleep better. But don't exercise right before you are about to go to bed.

Don't associate the bed with wakefulness. If you can't sleep, get up and read, sew, watch television, read a book, or write in a journal until you feel sleepy. Avoid sleeping pills and alcohol.

A good night's sleep is one of the most important parts of a wellness lifestyle and an essential component of being vibrantly healthy.

My body is relaxed and healthy,
overflowing with vitality.

Are You Rich?

Being rich implies so much more than having money. The true meaning of being rich is enjoying what you have. Once you understand this principle, getting more wealth becomes easier and even more enjoyable. Here are some aspects of being rich.

Living a balanced life. Is there a balance in your work and play, your labor and leisure? Do you take time out each day and week just for yourself to embrace the peace of your own company? This is being rich.

Caring. Living with compassion in thought and action is living with richness.

Enjoy. Live in the present moment and enjoy and delight in all your daily activities.

Contentment. This is not the fulfillment of what you want but the realization and gratitude of what you already have.

Opportunities. Look at everything that happens in your life as an opportunity to learn more about yourself and to be the best you can be. Choose a positive attitude.

The more I give, the more I am given to give.

Are You Rich? II

Health. Emerson said that "Health is our great-est wealth." Without your health, life seems chal-lenging and difficult. Do everything you can to make yourself healthy so you can create more richness in your life.

Happiness. When you realize that happiness is only found inside you, you will create richness.

Surrender. When we surrender our lives to God, we find everything we are seeking and our lives become masterpieces of richness.

Love. There is nothing more powerful to transform your life for the better than a consistent feeling of love. Love makes you rich. Love lifts your life to higher levels. Love creates miracles and opens to door to abundance, joy, fulfillment, happiness, peace and a magnificent life.

When you put all these ingredients together, you will live a life of richness.

Everywhere I look, I see opportunities to serve.

Resolving Conflicts with Children

Not all issues are worth fighting over with children and sometimes it's best to allow natural consequences to take over. The child who refuses to put his clothes in the hamper will one morning find he has no clean shirts to wear. If your daughter insists on wearing her shoes to bed, she'll probably discover that it's very uncomfortable and her feet get caught up in the sheets. As children grow up, they must take responsibility for their own behavior and learn from their own mistakes. Sometimes the hard way is the best way.

I radiate love to everyone I encounter;
my inner child celebrates life.

The Still, Small Voice

Prayer is the process of releasing the need and knowing that God is in charge. There is a feeling of peace because the stress of worry and concern has been lifted. Be receptive to divine inspiration no matter how it comes; signs and wonders can appear in the most unexpected ways.

God communicates through the still, small voice within each of us. You may know it as intuition or instinct, an insistent feeling or knowing that won't go away. A certain course of action just feels right. And the more you learn to trust this inner spiritual guidance, the more clearly you will recognize it. God is constantly sending guidance that points to your perfect path. Welcome it with an open heart and mind. When something is right for you, it comes or appears easily and effortlessly without struggle and it rides tandem with peace and joy.

I welcome God's guidance
with an open and grateful mind and heart.

Making Decisions

Daily life is filled with making decisions. Here's some advice that always works well. Move away from a problem when the same solution keeps coming up, but does not seem quite right intuitively. Also move away from a problem or challenge when you are feeling frustrated, having trouble concentrating, cannot focus clearly on the problem, feel irritable, stressed, or fatigued, or have trouble expressing your thoughts.

Take some sort of a break—a vacation, a day or a few hours off, or just some time alone in your office or home and breathe deeply—to develop inner calm, mental clarity, and a new sense of determination and positive attitude.

When one door closes, another door opens.
Everything I need is rushing to me now.

Prayer and Healing

In *Recovering the Soul,* author Dr. Larry Dossey describes a prayer study done by Randolph Byrd, a cardiologist. Dr. Byrd studied almost four hundred patients who were admitted to the coronary care unit of San Francisco General Hospital. Most of the patients had experienced an actual heart attack, or were suspected of having one. They were divided into two groups, both of whom received state of the art medical care. However, one group was prayed for while the other group was not. Their first names and a brief sketch of their conditions were given to various prayer groups throughout the United States.

When this study was over, the group which had received prayer was superior in several ways: they were far less likely to develop congestive heart failure; they were five times less likely to require antibiotics and three times less likely to need diuretics; none in the prayed for group required endotracheal intubation (breathing tube inserted in the throat); fewer of those in the prayed for group developed pneumonia; fewer of those who had received prayer experienced cardiopulmonary arrest, requiring resuscitation.

In your daily prayers, pray for others and not just for yourself.

Through God-in-me, all things are possible.

Change

The only constant or sure thing in life is change. The world is always changing. The courage to step out and try new things promises much continued progress and learning in your life.

It's exciting and interesting to be forever seeking out new methods and ideas. Explore all possibilities and listen to your intuition. That still, small voice inside will guide you on ways to live your life fully and will show you when to make changes.

I have the courage to step outside and try new things.

Reflective Communication

One of the greatest ways to support another person is to let him or her talk about their feelings and for you to listen carefully. When you help someone solve their own problems instead of giving advice all the time, you help build self-esteem and confidence in that person.

The first step is to listen. Occasionally repeat what the other person has said or what you thought they said. This can help them to stand outside themselves for a moment and be better able to find solutions.

Ask simple questions to lead the talker into examining his or her feelings or what may really be causing the feelings. If they can be lead to discovering the root of their problem, they will be closer to a solution.

Finally, listen and inquire without judgment or criticism. Be loving and supportive and let the person know you truly care about their well-being.

I choose to see others through the eyes of God.

Living Courageously

Encouragement is courage, strength from the heart. When you act from the heart, you act with courage. To do this, you have to be ready and willing to choose your dream. Take your dreams and act on them. Live as though your dream were your current reality. Hearten yourself to do what your inner guidance tells you to do. Courage comes from doing what you love.

Dream big, have courage, and follow the whisperings of your heart and inner guidance. When you dream and act, you'll discover that the courage you need has always been within you waiting to be called forth.

The more I act with courage and love,
the more courage and love I have to give.

Simplify Your Life

Simplification is to your life what a good reju-venation program is to your body; they both purify. You do not have to continually go faster and push harder in life. You have a choice. You are not a vic-tim of your environment. When you go faster and con-tinually push harder without keeping life in perspective, you grow insensitive to your needs and the needs of those around you.

Slow down. Take time to smell the flowers. Play more at this game called life. And be more concerned with your own integrity and your experience of life.

I let go and let God.

Commitment to Health

To be healthy, you must be committed. Making a commitment is one way to free yourself— your mind is no longer indecisive. Get past your excuses and follow through on what you said you were going to do. Make your word count. When you are committed, you honor your decision and allow nothing to deter you from reaching your goal. If you are ready for commitment, you will immediately arrange your personal circumstances so that your lifestyle totally supports your commitment. You will do whatever it takes, whatever you need to do, to order your life, let go of excess baggage and consciously focus on what is important.

New health habits thrive best in the company of friends who understand and appreciate your motive for change. Find a supportive friend or group with which to share and discuss your ideas.

By really committing yourself, by following though on your convictions and decisions, and allowing nothing to stand in the way of your becoming master of your life, you will gain tremendous power. When you are fully committed you will become master of your life and live fully.

I have all the energy I need
to accomplish my goals and fulfill my desires.

Positive Expectations

There is a group of cancer survivors at the Wellness Center in Santa Monica, California, who have lived past the time predicted for them by their physicians. The one thing they have in common is that they didn't deny the diagnosis, but they denied the verdict. They all have a blazing determination. Their expectations were not negative and that made a difference.

There is a connection between expectations and the immune system. Scientists are discovering that you can actually elevate levels of immune cell activities as a result of certain positive circumstances.

In a Harvard study, a group of people were shown a documentary on the work being done by Mother Teresa. After viewing a short twenty-minute movie, everyone's white blood cell function increased, showing improved immune functioning.

Do everything you can to support your immune system. Be positive and expect only the best in your life.

When I put my spiritual development first,
all of my other needs are fulfilled.

Eat Your Greens

If you've been looking for a way to boost the nutrients you get from your food, try greens. Greens are gaining recognition as a superior source of nutrients.

One of the reasons greens are important is the color itself. Chlorophyll, the pigment that makes plants green, receives its energy from the sun. In return, it manufactures the various chemicals needed for plant life. Scientifically, its composition closely resembles hemoglobin, the pigment that makes blood red. Chlorophyll helps to cleanse the body and has been used by physicians and dentists for years to successfully treat oral diseases, chronic ulcers, kidney stones, and acute infections of the upper respiratory tract and sinuses. Chlorophyll also protects the body against damage from radioactivity and substances that cause mutation. It is also believed that it may play an important future role in the prevention of cancer.

An easy way to take your greens is in the form of *KYO-GREEN* (see *Resources*). This delicious powdered drink is made from concentrated chlorella (an algae loaded with vitamins, minerals, and protein) juice, young barley and wheat grass, brown rice, and kelp— all excellent sources of chlorophyll. Make it an important part of your health program.

*I eat greens daily to provide
my body temple with superior nutrition.*

Laughter Heals

When was the last time you laughed deep down in your belly? Laughter is the lubricant of life. It alleviates anxiety and lightens depression and helps heal your body and make it healthy.

Laughter releases a variety of hormones and other natural and beneficial chemicals in your body. When you laugh, the right side of the brain connected with creativity and emotion is more active. Endocrine glands are also affected by laughter. Natural painkillers like endorphins and enkephalins are released from the pituitary gland when you laugh. The adrenals secrete epinephrine, norepinephrine, and dopamine, which give that glow after you've had a good laugh. The catecholamines released from the adrenals also help to fight the pain and inflammation of conditions such as arthritis.

Laughter also improves blood flow and lowers blood pressure because the arteries become more relaxed. During a good belly laugh, virtually every organ of the body gets a good workout. Is it any wonder that laughter has been called the best medicine?

I laugh my way to health and happiness.

The Challenge

The major degenerative diseases that plague North Americans—hypertension, obesity, atherosclerosis leading to heart attack and stroke, adult-onset diabetes mellitus, and even varieties of inflammatory arthritis—are being shown to have major nutritional components. Many of these diseases can be prevented, arrested, and even reversed by appropriate food and lifestyle choices. However, seventy-seven percent of the US. medical schools require no formal nutrition education of their graduates, thus physicians often find themselves inadequately prepared to provide the dietary guidance that can make the difference between therapeutic success or failure.

Increasingly, health professionals are seeking continuing education in the basic sciences and clinical applications of nutrition. If you are a health professional, look into taking an accredited seminar emphasizing how important patients' diet can be as a key determinant of health and as an effective therapeutic tool.

I am always paying attention
to my inner doctor for guidance.

Fruit Force

When you bite into a piece of fresh, ripe fruit, your taste buds are flooded with seductive flavors. Fruit is juicy and sweet (the sugar in fruit is sweeter than table sugar) and very healthy.

Not only can a diet rich in fruit boost your exercise performance by replenishing precious nutrients and fluids drained by perspiration, it can protect your health by helping to prevent heart disease, strokes, high blood pressure, cataracts, and cancer. Just two to four pieces (or two to four half cup servings) of fruit daily can be enough to have you reaping these very sweet rewards. It's hard to believe that something so tasty can pack such nutritional punch.

Small nutritious meals are very satisfying to me.

Toning Your Muscles

Here are some exercises you can do today and everyday.

Whole Body Stretch: Standing with feet hip-width apart, toes pointing forward, knees slightly bent, reach for the sky ten times. Drop your chin to your chest and roll forward, letting the weight of your head pull you slowly down as far as is comfortable. Unroll back up, pulling the tailbone down and keeping knees bent throughout. Repeat this sequence three times.

Abdominal: Lie on your back, knees bent to chest, fingers laced behind your head. Exhale as you slowly curl your tailbone and head toward each other. Inhale as you return. Start with ten and build by tens to a hundred.

Outer Thigh and Buttocks: Lie on your side, head relaxed on your arm, legs bent at ninety degrees, as if you were sitting in a straight chair. Exhale and raise top leg slowly in four count (about six inches, directly above bottom leg) and inhale as you lower it in four counts. Do four times. Then do faster (two counts up and two down) eight times, then faster yet for sixteen quick counts. Inhale and bring knee of top leg to chest, then exhale and extend leg, foot flexed, in a straight line with your spine. Do eight times. Keeping top leg straight and in line with your spine, knee facing forward, exhale and raise leg. Inhale and lower. Do sixteen times. Switch sides and repeat with other leg.

Exercise is fun to me
and I eagerly look forward to it every day.

Let's Go Biking

Bikes now come in shapes and styles specifically designed to meet the needs of a variety of terrains and riding demands. To help you decide, here's a rundown of three basic types:

Road Bikes: The most specialized kind around, road bikes are intended for long distance touring trips and competitive races. Their function is speed, so the frame is lightweight and very aerodynamic. The curved handlebars allow for two different hand positions and most come with either fourteen or twenty-one speeds; if hills are a major part of your riding terrain, look for a model with twenty-one speeds.

Mountain Bikes: Although these sturdy, heavy, wide-tired bikes are designed for off-road riding and rugged terrain, most buyers ride them in town as well. The bike's sturdy frame and wide tires make people feel more secure. These are not good bikes for riding long distances—the weight of the bike and width of the tires will wear you out faster. Most have twenty-one speeds.

Hybrid Bikes: Combining the lightness of a road bike with a sturdier frame and wider tires, hybrids are perfect for the recreational cycler. They work well on-road and are better than heavy mountain bikes for long distances, and while they're not rugged enough for serious rock-jumping, hybrids can handle off-road paths and trails. Twenty-one speeds are standard on most of these bikes.

The Klein company makes excellent bikes (see *Resources*).

I always find the time to exercise during the day.

The Top Ten Grains

These top ten grains help to fight heart disease, cancer, and extra pounds. They were rated by the Center for Science in the Public Interest for fiber and five nutrients—magnesium, B6, zinc, copper, and iron. Here are the results in descending order.

Quinoa: It's a good source of iron and copper.

Amaranth: This is high in protein and a great source of fiber, iron, and copper.

Buckwheat groats: If you roast buckwheat before you boil it, you've got Kasha. Rich in copper, magnesium, and fiber.

Bulgur: Wheat kernels (berries) that have been steamed, dried, and cracked into small pieces. Look for brown color. High in fiber and magnesium.

Barley: Get unpearled (brown) barley because it's higher in fiber and iron.

Wild rice: Mix it with brown rice. Rich in B6, fiber, and magnesium.

Millet: Delicious and filled with magnesium and copper.

Brown rice: The only rice that has vitamin E and has much more fiber than white rice.

Triticale: A cross between wheat and rye with more protein than either of its parent grains and lots of magnesium and fiber.

Wheat berries: Add to your brown and wild rice for variety. A good source of fiber.

Several times each week I eat a variety of grains to be optimally healthy.

Eating Less Fat

When you eat less fat, you will feel a difference immediately. Each time you eat a fatty meal, your red blood cells clump together, moving slowly through the circulatory system and clogging up capillaries. This deprives your brain of oxygen, resulting in grogginess. But when you stop eating such meals, your red cells return to normal, and your capillaries open up. The result is that you feel calmer and more energetic, you sleep better, and your complexion improves. And at the same time a subtler but even more important change is taking place within your body. The fatty plaques inside your arteries shrink and your immune system grows stronger.

In all my food choices, I select foods low in fat.
I am radiantly healthy and celebrate this gift of life.

Smart Eating

One of the most potent weapons in the battle against aging and disease is diet. The foods you put into your body and those you avoid, how much and perhaps even when you eat, all have an impact on longevity. By following the American Heart Association's guidelines of eating less fat and salt, more fresh fruit, vegetables, and whole grains, you can reduce the risks of heart disease, cancer, and obesity. The most radical dietary researchers believe that by *reducing caloric intake,* people could live significantly longer—*up to 150 years.* Here are some of the suggestions on how to eat better to live longer.

Eat a variety of fruits and vegetables, and lots of them.

Eat less fat.

Stop dieting and quit yo-yoing with your weight.

Eat dinner at lunch time.

If you can't have just one, don't drink alcohol at all. Better yet, don't drink at all.

Join the breakfast club. Have a healthy breakfast each morning.

Don't overeat.

Emphasize complex carbohydrate and lots of fiber in your diet.

Nurture your self-esteem.

Make your health a top priority in your life.

Today I renew my commitment to being healthy and resolve to make my word count.

Overcoming Jet Lag

While scientific thinking on minimizing jet lag emphasizes exposing the eyes to light at precisely calculated intervals, physical activity, a jog or a brisk walk may be another potent anti jet lag tool. The strongest effect may be achieved when activity and light exposure are combined. The next time you are crossing time zones, try jogging or exercising in the sun to clear travel-induced fatigue or cobwebs.

I have an abundance of energy
and my body is filled with vitality.

Children's Diets

Children continue to eat a less than perfect diet, according to a study conducted at the University of Minnesota at St. Paul. Nutrient intakes for children, ages two to ten years old, were compared for the years 1978 and 1988. Results showed that although calorie, protein, carbohydrate, and fat intakes remained constant during the ten-year span, vitamin and mineral intakes decreased, suggesting that children are consuming more calorie-dense, nutrient-poor foods. More than half of the children studied consumed less than the Recommended Dietary Allowances (RDAs) for several vitamins and minerals, including calcium, vitamin B6, and zinc.

Despite growing awareness of the importance of vitamin and mineral status in the prevention of disease today and in the future, children's diets and nutrient intakes are not improving and are actually worse than they were ten years ago.

*I nurture my inner child by being healthy
and not taking myself or my life too seriously.*

Choose Your Doctor Carefully

Choose your doctor carefully and make sure it is one that listens to you. There is a tendency for doctors to turn to technology and all kinds of elaborate testing first and the human ears second. A powerful combination is what the doctor can do for you and how you can help the doctor in what you can do for yourself.

Take great care of yourself so you don't get sick. Eat healthy foods, exercise regularly, find times to rest and relax, and think positive thoughts. It's also essential to find some time to be alone every day so you can turn within and pay attention to what your higher self is telling you.

Take loving care of your body, pamper it and nurture it. Get massages and other types of body work done on a regular basis. Massages are an excellent way to relieve stress, take away tension, and to soothe your entire body. When your body is relaxed and healthy, then your immune system can work more efficiently to keep you finely tuned and functioning optimally.

My body is healed, rejuvenated, and filled with energy, light, and love.

High Five for Fitness Enthusiasts

Did you have your five servings of fruits and vegetables today or yesterday? Here are some reasons you need to get in at least five servings daily, especially if you workout regularly.

Fruits and vegetables provide vitamins and minerals, which you need for growth, healing, resistance, healthy skin and hair, electrolyte replacement, nerve conduction, and even muscle contraction. You get quicker energy from fruits, longer-lasting energy from vegetables. Fiber keeps you regular, helps prevent bloating, and fills your stomach so you eat less fatty food. Fiber also helps prevent cancer, and certain fibers help lower cholesterol.

Today I choose to take extra special care of myself and listen to the whisperings of my heart.

Chlorophyll

Chlorophyll is the green coloring of plants. Scientific studies have found chlorophyll to be an excellent nutritional supplement offering numerous benefits for the body. Chlorophyll builds high blood count, detoxifies the body, promotes digestive and dental health, prevents internal and external infections, helps purify the liver and other organs, promotes healthy skin, and eliminates bad breath and body odor.

The DeSouza Company (see *Resources*) makes a top quality 100 percent liquid chlorophyll to use daily. They also offer a line of chlorophyll personal care products including tooth powder and gel, mouth rinse and spray, and a natural moisturizing lotion. All these items are available in your health food store.

I am grateful for my life.

Stronger Legs

Here's a very easy and effective way to strengthen and tone the muscles in your front thigh. It works best if you have some ankle weights. Put them on, sit on a high stool or counter (or stack a few telephone books on a regular chair so your feet don't touch the ground).

With knee bent, rotate left leg from your hip so that your toes point outward, then lift your ankle until your leg is fully extended (without locking your knee joint). Slowly lower to starting position.

Rotate your leg from your hip until your toes point forward and lift again. Slowly lower.

Rotate your leg until your toes face inward, lift and lower. Repeat these three sets with the other leg.

An easier version: Use light weights, if needed.

The easiest version: Don't use any weights.

My legs are strong and toned
and I have an abundance of energy.

Wonder Foods

Ginger: This spice is a natural diet aid, possibly boosting the rate at which the body burns calories. It also helps nausea, whether from car or sea sickness or morning sickness. In addition, ginger helps to quell indigestion. Take a slice of ginger and put it through your juicer when making fresh juice. A combination of carrot, parsley, celery, and ginger is wonderful—also a great drink for your immune system.

Oats: This grain is a good choice for lowering LDL cholesterol. Recent studies found that eating three grams of soluble fiber a day, the amount in a large bowl of one hundred percent oat bran cereal, can cut LDL cholesterol by at least 5.6 percent in six weeks.

Orange juice: The best is freshly made orange juice from your juicer. This is a classic source of vitamin C with folic acid, which helps prevent birth defects and may protect against cervical cancer. Freshly made, raw citrus juices also contain limonoids, substances that studies shows can activate detoxifying enzymes in the body, possibly cutting cancer risk. Smokers may want a double dose of orange juice: their vitamin C requirement is twice that of nonsmokers. When making juice, a favorite combination is a third grapefruit, a third orange, and a third tangerine.

I celebrate the wonder and beauty of nature.

The Power of Raw Foods

Do you want to be free from disease, obesity, fatigue, and failing health? Consider eating more of your foods raw. A tremendous proliferation of white blood cells occurs whenever cooked food is eaten. When raw food is eaten, there is no substantial increase in the number of white blood cells.

In *Survival Into the 21st Century*, author Victoras Kulvinskas states, "Cooking does not improve the nutritional value of food. It destroys or makes unavailable eighty-five percent of the original nutrients." Additional studies of protein by the Max Plank Institute for Nutritional Research in Germany have found that cooked proteins have only fifty percent bio-availability when compared to uncooked proteins.

Although cooking and conventional food preparation represent destructive agents to the nutritive elements of food, these factors must be put into proper perspective relative to all other factors of a healthful lifestyle. A pure raw food diet is not necessarily the best diet for everyone. Strive to eat at least half of your diet raw and see how you feel.

I express health and vitality in everything I do.

Exercising after You Eat

A moderate (not high intensity) walk after a meal gives you a fat burning bonus. If you take a brisk three-mile walk on an empty stomach, you'll burn about 300 calories. But if you're walking on a full stomach, you not only burn those 300 calories—you also burn another fifteen percent of that total. Exercising after eating seems to give it a double boost, so it overcompensates and burns more calories than it needs to. Make sure to keep your postmeal workouts low intensity.

I exercise my right to be happy and think positively.

Energy Food

If you workout at least two hours a day, five or more times each week, you will find that the foods you eat before, during, and after a workout have a profound effect on your training. Before and after a workout, the best food is an easily digestible meal such as fresh fruit or complex carbohydrates that are a good source of antioxidants, vitamins, and minerals to speed recovery and muscle repair. Protein is also important in repairing tissues and building muscle. Branched chain amino acids (BCAAs) from protein can directly supply energy to muscle, as well as spare its breakdown, for energy.

After an intense workout there is a window of time in which recovery and muscle repair is fastest. During the first sixty to ninety minutes after exercise, nutrients can be used more quickly and efficiently to restore glycogen (the muscles' energy supply) and repair and build muscle.

While a bowl of cereal, a piece of fresh fruit, vitamins, minerals, and extra BCAAs are a good pre or post workout meal, sometimes you may not have meal preparation time. A quick alternative may be a well designed food bar such as PowerBar (see *Resources*). PowerBar has the benefits of the quick energy from fruit, sustained energy from complex carbohydrates, protein and BCAAs for muscle energy and repair, antioxidants, vitamins, and minerals. Two favorite flavors are Wild Berry and Cinnamon Apple.

I choose foods which provide
energy, repair, and healing.

An Apple and Carrot a Day

Apples, like many fruits and vegetables, contain the fiber that's necessary to keep your digestive system healthy. Diets high in fiber have been linked with a lowered risk of colon cancer. While scientists aren't exactly sure why this is, they do know that insoluble fiber moves foods through the digestive tract more quickly. It decreases the transit time and therefore anything harmful is in contact with the bowel for a shorter period of time.

When it comes to carrots, you can't get much better in terms of an abundance of beta-carotene, an antioxidant that is converted into vitamin A in the body. Like all antioxidants, beta-carotene—found in deep yellow and dark green vegetables—is believed to aid in preventing disease. Other high beta-carotene sources include apricots, cantaloupe, bok choy, spinach, sweet potatoes, Swiss chard, yams, and dark green leafy vegetables.

Each day I choose to eat
a variety of different colored foods.

Choosing to Exercise

Once-a-week exercise lowers the risk of adult-onset (type II) diabetes by as much as twenty-three percent. Vigorous exercise from two to four times a week reduces a person's risk of developing diabetes by thirty-eight percent; at five times or more per week, the risk is cut by forty-two percent. By living a healthy lifestyle and exercising regularly, you can protect yourself from a life-threatening disease. Lack of exercise contributes to as many as one of four cases of type II diabetes.

Appropriate physical activity can also protect inflamed joints and maintain range of motion. For severe cases of arthritis, isometric exercises and gentle movements are best. For people with less inflammation, swimming, walking, and stationary cycling are appropriate. The activities to avoid are high-impact sports that require running and jumping.

Exercise is one of the many ways
I love and respect myself.

Rest and Relaxation

Rest is Nature's great restorative process, just as activity and excitement represent her great exhaustive process. Activity is an essential part of life but must be alternated with period of rest or else you wear yourself down.

In life, two simultaneous processes are in continuous operation. The first process is growth, development, and replenishment. This is called anabolism and is dominant during periods of rest and sleep. The other process involves wear and tear and is called catabolism which is dominant in periods of activity. Collectively, these two processes constitute metabolism. Neither of these processes is ever entirely passive during life.

Pay attention to your body's signals. If you are tired, exhausted, or lack energy, you probably need to rest and sleep more. Take one day a week, three consecutive days each month and a few days with each change of season to rest more, to get away from as much exterior stimuli as possible to rest body, mind, and spirit.

Your body is always talking to you and telling you what it needs. Pay attention and make sure you are getting enough sleep and rest.

I pay attention to the messages my body is giving me to rest and I enjoy the peace of my own company.

Eating for Life

Populations living on a starch-based diet, as our ancestors did, have little or none of the heart disease and cancer so common in "civilized" countries. And today, a growing weight of undeniable evidence indicates that a low fat, low or no animal protein, low sugar, high natural carbohydrate, primarily vegetarian diet is optimal for a healthier, more energetic, longer life. And yet, millions of Americans sicken and die prematurely each year because they resist changing their diets, getting more exercise, or quitting smoking. They avoid a conscious choice based on available facts by using a variety of psychological defense mechanisms: I don't worry about high cholesterol; I like smoking; I'm entitled to one vice; nobody lives forever; maybe tomorrow I'll quit eating junk food.

Consciously choose your own lifestyle and take a realistic look at the consequences of your actions. Let's not pretend the consequences don't exist or that they won't happen to us. Make your choices consciously, free of illusions, wishes, or denial. Maintaining your illusions can be hazardous to your health.

I am fully committed to being healthy
and living my highest potential.

Go Away Bugs

You can fight bug's attraction to your body all year long with geranium oil, the green alternative to bug spray. A homemade lotion with proportions of four teaspoons of soy oil to sixteen drops of geranium oil massaged into the skin should repel insects just as well as most over-the-counter pesticides.

You can also leave a tissue or cloth sprinkled with a few drops of the oil by the bedside to keep bugs at bay all night.

I bless all insects and send them on their way.

Fruit Facts

FRUIT	CALORIES	GOOD SOURCE OF ...
Apple, 1 medium	80	pectin (a cholesterol-lowering fiber)
Apricots, 3 medium	50	beta-carotene
Banana, 1 medium	100	potassium
Berries, 1 cup (all kinds)	75	fiber, potassium, vitamin C
Cherries, 10	50	potassium
Cranberries, 1 cup	45	fiber
Dates, 5	110	fiber, potassium
Grapes, 1 cup	60	potassium
Guava, 1 medium	45	potassium, vitamin C
Kiwifruit, 1 medium	50	fiber, vitamin C, potassium
Kumquats, 5 medium	60	fiber, vitamin C
Mango, 1 medium	135	beta-carotene, potassium, vitamin C
Melons, Cantaloupe, Crenshaw, 1/2	80	beta-carotene, potassium, vitamin C

*I eat foods that nourish my body and mind
and boost my self-esteem.*

Fruit Facts II

FRUIT	CALORIES	GOOD SOURCE OF ...
Orange, 1 medium	60	potassium, vitamin C
Papaya, 1 medium	100	beta-carotene, potassium, vitamin C
Peach, 1 medium	40	beta-carotene
Pear, 1 medium	90	potassium
Persimmon, 1 medium	110	beta-carotene, fiber, potassium
Pineapple, 1 cup	80	vitamin
Plums, 2 medium	70	potassium
Strawberries, 1 cup	45	potassium, vitamin C
Tangerine, 1 medium	37	vitamin C

*Fresh juices and nutritious meals
are very satisfying to me.*

Alternate Nostril Breathing

You can practice this very effective breathing technique every day if you wish. In this exercise you inhale through one nostril, retain the breath, then exhale through the other nostril. Healthy people actually do breathe predominately first through one nostril and then the other, alternating every couple of hours. This focused alternate nostril breathing helps balance the use of both hemispheres of the brain and increases concentration.

Exhale completely, breathe in through the left nostril holding the right closed with your right thumb.

Hold the breath, closing both nostrils.

Breathe out through the right nostril, keeping the left closed with your ring finger.

Breathe in through the right nostril, keeping the left closed.

Hold the breath, closing both nostrils.

Breathe out through the left nostril, keeping the right closed with your thumb.

Practice this for ten minutes daily, every day for a week. You'll noticed a positive difference in how you feel.

With each breath I take, I center my thoughts on being loving and peaceful.

The Key to Health and Happiness

Our sense of happiness and well-being is greatly influenced by the presence or absence of certain chemicals and hormones in the bloodstream. Brisk or aerobic exercise such as swimming, cycling, brisk walking, jogging, stepping, and rowing stimulates the production of the two chemicals in the body, norepinephrine and enkephalin, that are known to lift spirits.

Most people can ban the blues with a simple, vigorous ten minute exercise session three times a week. Ten minutes of exercise will double the body's level of norepinephrine, and the effect is long-lasting. Norepinephrine would seem to be the chemical key to happiness.

Not only does exercise give you a more positive attitude about yourself and life, but if you get on a regular exercise regime, circumstances in life that would normally bother or challenge you lose their pull. You gain a higher perspective on life and strengthen your ability to understand what's really important in life.

I celebrate the joy of life by keeping active
and exercising regularly.

Slowing the Aging Process

If you are physically active over a lifetime, you will age at a slower rate than someone who is sedentary.

What you do during your twenties, thirties, and forties will help determine your health and stamina in later years. By working out aerobically now, you'll boost the power of your heart, lungs and circulatory system, lowering your risk of heart disease, high cholesterol levels, and hypertension.

With strength training exercise (weight training), you'll maintain the size and power of your muscles, keep your metabolism high and gain less fat. Strength training and aerobic exercise also help preserve bone density, reducing the incidence of osteoporosis, stooping and fractures later on. By using and stretching the tendons and ligaments surrounding joints now, you'll stave off stiffness and immobility.

And even if you're in your fifties, sixties, seventies or more, it's never to late to start. Everything you do to stay active will make a positive difference in your health and life.

My muscles, bones, heart, and every part of my body radiate health and vitality.

Food Facts

Ounce for ounce, broccoli florets contain nearly eight times as much beta-carotene as the stalks. But don't discard the stalks; like the florets, they contain calcium, fiber, vitamin C, and other nutrients.

Because of their high oil content, seeds and nuts should be kept dry and in the refrigerator to prevent rancidity.

Too much refined sugar in your diet will be transformed by the liver into fat and stored in the fat deposits of the body. Scientists have also discovered a relationship between sugar consumption and heart attacks.

Always select foods which support your well-being. How and what you eat reflects how you feel about yourself.

I choose to take loving care of my precious body by eating only healthy, natural foods.

Paramahansa Yogananda

Paramahansa Yogananda founded the Self-Realization Fellowship (SRF) in 1920 in order to teach the scientific principles of meditation (see *Resources*). SRF believes in the brotherhood of all people, that we have one common Father, and that all true paths lead to the same God. All religions are respected.

Yogananda's book, *The Autobiography of a Yogi*, shows a different way to live—that it is possible to control your thoughts, emotions, and live a spirit-filled (hence peaceful, joyful, happy) life. Yogananda teaches how important it is to spend time in meditation every day and to live your life in the presence of God. His home study lessons cover meditation, his philosophy, and how to live fully—physically, mentally, emotionally, and spiritually.

My life is a harmonious expression
of the insights and values of my higher self.

Improving Your Love Life

To have a good love life, you must feel comfortable about your body. Appreciate your body and that of your partner as sexy and attractive. You will look sexy when you feel sexy. Focus on getting in touch with your sexual feelings.

Think sexy. A body that feels sensual is a beautiful body, no matter what shape or size. You're as beautiful as you feel and act—especially when it comes to engaging in loving sex with your partner.

My body is sexy and beautiful.

Make a Stand

Make a stand and be committed to yourself for your health and happiness; to your brothers and sisters for equal rights and justice; to all living things and the environment for good Mother Earth; and to God, knowing you are always one. With this partnership, anything and everything is possible.

You wake up to a whole new world every morning. Today is brand new. Today can be a new beginning where you can start fresh. Today is in sequence with all the yesterdays that preceded it, but it is not bound by them. You have a choice.

You don't have to be the same person today that you were yesterday. You can choose your direction and your response every conscious moment of your life. You're not a robot, and you are not a slave. And you don't have to be a creature of habit.

Today make a stand for what you want and commit to it.

I am changing and transforming
my old and limiting beliefs.

Let There Be Light

A reasonable and moderate amount of sunlight can do much good for your well-being. It is no exaggeration to say that sunlight has enormous benefits to health. The sun naturally tends to lower blood pressure, strengthens the heart, lowers cholesterol, stabilizes the blood sugar, and increases energy, endurance, and muscular strength. Sunlight also increases your resistance to infection, and enhances the production of hormones.

Sunlight activates the production of vitamin D in the skin and vitamin D is made from cholesterol. The more vitamin D formed in your skin from exposure to sunlight, the more cholesterol you use up.

Don't be afraid of a little sunshine, just be careful about it. Never allow yourself to get red, or even to develop a dark tan, because these are indications of skin damage.

One of the first things you discover in life is that sunshine feels good on your body. If you enjoy the sun moderately and carefully, it will boost your health.

Whether the sun is shining or not,
I feel its light shining in my heart.

Inspire Yourself

Who are the people that inspire you the most? Which men or women do you know personally or can read about who have set goals, overcome adversity and great challenges, and have accomplished what most people would think impossible? Let them be your teachers. Put your heart into everything you do and don't work on things that don't have your heart.

Spend some time everyday and listen to audiocassettes that motivate and inspire you to live on higher ground. You can do this at home, in your car, and sometimes at work, depending on where you work. Let your mind soak up all the ingredients you need to become the master of your life and create your highest vision.

Everyone I meet is a teacher to me
reminding me to practice love and forgiveness.

Living by Inner Guidance

Peace Pilgrim (see *Resources*) had such an innocent simplicity about her, she touched everyone she met. She was a beautiful channel for God and had a childlike faith in God, knowing that all her needs would be met.

Someone once asked her if there was indeed a guidance beyond ourselves. She answered, "We all have tremendous guidance, but especially those who are willing to allow their lives to be governed by the high nature. You see, that higher nature is there and to a certain extent you receive some guidance, but if you allow it to govern your life (and you have free will as to whether you will allow it to govern your life or not); then, of course, you will receive constant guidance. Our lives are ordered and arranged for us in many wonderful ways if we allow it to happen."

I let go and allow God
to take charge of my life and affairs.

Take Time to Play

Play more at this game of life. Be more concerned with your own integrity and experience of living than how you look to people. When was the last time you played? The last time you ran until you felt warm wind streaming across your face? Or felt the water rush around you and caress your body as you swam? Be active and happy, and love your body and what it can do.

Don't lose the sheer joy, laughter, and lightheartedness of play. Find ways of re-introducing play into your busy days and fitness routines that will make your life happier, workouts more fun, and make you and your exercise more productive.

Today and everyday,
I let my inner child come out play and celebrate life.

We Are Blessed

Remember how blessed you are each and every day. You have come to this place in your life and have the power and ability to make your life anything you want it to be. If things or circumstances aren't pleasant and peaceful right now, you can exercise your power to change them.

Take any negative condition in your life and be willing to see it differently. When you are willing to see your problem differently, just face it and ask the higher power within you to reveal some alternative ways you could see this person, situation, or condition. Be willing to have your judgment of the problem proven false. *Be willing to forgive everything and everyone involved, including yourself.* As you become the least bit willing, you release the power that harmonizes, transforms, heals, and resurrects.

I let go and let my inner guidance orchestrate
my day and all my affairs.

Preventing Lower Back Problems

You can help prevent lower back problems on road trips by not unloading luggage immediately upon destination arrival. Get out and move around a bit first to let contracted muscles reactivate. Stretch your arms to the sky; do some slow side bends; swing your arms gently side to side; pull your knees to your chest one at a time. After a few minutes of such wake-up stretching, you'll be ready to attack the trunk. Try to keep the luggage close to your body when you lift. Don't lift with an outstretched arm.

If you frequently travel long distances by car, you should do exercises for your abdominal muscles regularly at home. The majority of lower back problems are caused by having weak abdominal muscles.

For every hour you drive, pull over to the side of the road and take at least five minutes to stretch. Stretch to the sky, walk around, twist at your waist, breathe deeply, and always bless your automobile.

I am grateful for my means of transportation
and I always arrive safely at my destination.

Nature's Alarm Clock

Sleep researchers have known that the body is equipped with some kind of biological clock, but they didn't know what it was programmed to do. Neuroscientists have determined that the clock is really an alarm, a wake up call that's programmed into a tiny cluster of nerve cells in the brain.

This built-in wake up signal is the reason jet lag sufferers have such a hard time sleeping through the night in a new time zone. Regardless of how many hours they have stayed awake, and no matter how sleepy they are, when that biological alarm clock goes off, the exhausted traveler wakes up and stays up.

Jet lag is an example of the conflict between the natural alarm clock and the drive to catch up on missed sleep, a process known as sleep homeostasis. Over the hours, the signal gradually weakens, which allows one to eventually go to sleep.

I fall asleep effortlessly and wake up feeling refreshed and ready to greet my day and celebrate life.

Living Peacefully

Be grateful for every thought and action in your life. Have a consistent attitude of gratitude.

Take time each day to quiet your mind and reflect on the here and now.

Make living peacefully a top priority in your life. Be committed to living peacefully.

Remember what's really important in life.

Ask your inner guidance for assistance all the time. Live with patience.

Find ways to serve others whenever possible.

Spend time in nature several times each week.

Nothing can impinge on the peace that is earned through knowing and loving the self.

Simplify your life.

Know in your heart you can handle and overcome anything. Just pay attention to the whisperings of your heart.

When inner peace is sought after and found, there is a kind of magic that occurs in the outer world and life no longer seems threatening.

Practice seeing all life around you as an aspect of yourself.

I rest in peace, love, and confidence
with God as my Source.

Positive Reinforcement

Praise people's achievements and they'll work harder and happier.

Post a piece of paper in a visible spot (bulletin board, refrigerator door, or mirror). Title it "I Saw Someone Doing His/Her Best."

Whenever you see someone else trying his or her hardest, write it down on the sheet of paper. (I saw Pamela working hard to meet her deadline; I saw Helen practicing for her presentation; I saw Gary creating the time to get in his workout at the gym.)

Give special recognition (special badge, gift certificate) whenever someone works extra hard to do his or her best on a project.

Remember, the important thing is to praise the effort. It doesn't matter if the person wins or loses in other people's eyes.

I find ways to show my acceptance and appreciation
for myself and others.

Visiting Your Doctor

When you see a doctor, be sure to mention the symptom that bothers you the most *first.* The symptom you mention first is probably the symptom your doctor will pay the most attention to. You should go to your doctor with a written list of your symptoms, listed in order of concern to you. When you first see your doctor, say, "I have a list here of (whatever number) concerns, listed in order." You can read from the list, or hand the list to your doctor.

Most patients go to the doctor with several problems, and that they tend to mention the symptom that concerns them the most last, often when the doctor is about to leave the exam room. If your doctor understands that you have a specific number of concerns in an order that's important to you, there's a greater likelihood you'll leave his or her office with all your questions answered.

God loves me so much and makes me whole.

Pets Make You Healthy

Pet owners are healthier than people who do not own pets. Pet owners have lower cholesterol and triglyceride levels than non-owners. They are also less likely to suffer from nervousness, insomnia, stomachaches, headaches, and other minor health problems.

It's also interesting to note that new pet owners, especially dog owners, experience increases in psychological well being and self-esteem. Consider opening your home to more animal friends.

All animals have something to tell or teach me if I just pay attention.

Love and Intimacy

Sexual love and intimacy are the first things shunted aside when work pressures, fatigue, unfinished business, and self-absorption get in the way of a couple's intimacy and arousal. It helps if you become emotionally available by sharing feelings about work or fatigue with your partner. Focus on the sensuality and playfulness of lovemaking instead of viewing sex and intimacy as a task and worrying about goals and performance while in bed.

I enjoy expressing my sexuality.
I deserve to be happy and fulfilled.

Fabric Danger

Formaldehyde resin used to keep no-iron linens, permanent press clothing, and polyester/cotton fabrics wrinkle free emits formaldehyde fumes for the life of the fabric, which could be years. There are some recognizable symptoms of formaldehyde vapor inhalation: tiredness, headaches, coughing, watery eyes, and respiratory problems.

Buy only natural fibers, which are generally not treated with formaldehyde. Avoid fabrics with labels reading "easy care one hundred percent cotton" or "no-iron cotton," which could mean formaldehyde finishes.

I love my body and treat it like royalty.

Never Relinquish Your Dreams

If there's something you want, don't give up. Persevere and have faith. Sometimes it takes longer than expected to achieve a goal but if it's very important to you, it's worth the wait.

Author of the Declaration of Independence, founder of the University of Virginia, and our nation's third president, Thomas Jefferson was a brilliant man. He also believed in never relinquishing your dreams.

Jefferson was a young man when he first conceived of founding a university. But not until the eighth decade of his life was he able to realize this ambitious dream. Long after other men or women would have given up, and despite long years of frustration and affliction with heart disease, Jefferson pursued his goal with a zeal and enthusiasm that belied his older age and ultimately triumphed.

Don't relinquish your dreams. Believe in yourself and your ability to live your highest vision.

I am attracting the people, circumstances, and finances to make my dreams come true.

Know Your Credit

For a free copy of your credit report, write to TRW and include your full name (with middle initial), addresses for the last five years, Social Security number, year of birth, and, if married, your spouse's name. Also include a copy of a document that links your name and address, such as a utility bill or your driver's license to prevent release of data to unauthorized persons. Send this information to TRW Consumer Assistance, Box 2350, Chatsworth, CO 91313.

People find errors on their TRW. You'll never know if you don't request a copy. You don't have to wait until you're filling out a loan application for a car or house to check your TRW. Check every year just to make sure there are no errors.

There is more than enough to go around for everyone, including me.

Money Talk

Would you like to clear up your debts and start saving more money? Take all credit cards, except one for emergencies, out of your wallet. Consider cutting up all cards except one as a way to limit spending. Cancel multiple Visa and Master Cards. Don't let them become a way to finance your daily living. Make a list of your outstanding credit card debts. Pay them off one at a time. Celebrate when you finish paying off the outstanding debt by cutting your card in half. When making a payment on your credit card, always pay more the minimum requirement. Even if it is $10 to $100 more, in the long run, it will save you lots of money and expedite your goal of paying it off.

Don't carry your checkbook around. Write yourself one allowance check every week for lunches, magazines, newspapers, groceries, cleaning, and movies. Become your own banker and learn how to be self-disciplined. When you get your paycheck, immediately take ten percent, before paying any bills, and put it away in a special savings account.

See yourself prospering in everything you do. Affirm and accept that you are an abundant being, worthy and deserving of the best life has to offer. Be grateful that you are abundant and can save your income easily and effortlessly.

God-in-me is my unlimited, overflowing supply of every kind of good.

Falling Asleep Easily

Difficulty falling asleep, or awakening in the middle of the night and being unable to return to sleep, is a common problem. Typical causes of insomnia are smoking, caffeine, overeating, lack of exercise, physical tension, excessive mental stimulation, or worry.

To increase the likelihood of falling into a sound sleep, avoid stimulants like coffee, spices, and alcohol. Also avoid eating three hours before going to bed. Include low fat, calcium-rich foods. Calcium has a calming effect on the nervous system. Include some broccoli, collards, kale, mustard greens, or carrots in your diet. Just before bedtime, drink a cup of chamomile tea, which acts as a mild sedative.

To reduce tension prior to bedtime, practice the following relaxation exercise. Lie comfortably on your back with a pillow underneath your knees. Breathe rhythmically and deeply in a relaxed manner. Visualize your feet. Tense your toes and feet, then suddenly relax. Do the same with your calves: visualize, tense, then relax. Do the same in sequence for your thighs, buttocks, stomach, chest, shoulders, hands, forearms, biceps, neck, and face. At the end of this exercise, you should feel relaxed and ready to drop off to sleep.

I give my body what it wants to be healthy and whole.

Becoming a Winner

Why is it that winners and successful people in life tend to win? The reason is that basic attitudes toward life influence the way people handle what happens to them. The unconscious mind merely stores data, which is edited and has values placed on it before it becomes conscious. As a result, the minds of people embracing positive mental attitudes constantly work to create positive self-esteem points from any event or thought.

Monitor your thoughts and visions and choose to possess a positive mental attitude regardless of your past or appearances. What you think about and believe today will be what you create and experience tomorrow.

I am a channel for creativity and success.

Let Go of Blame

One of the greatest healers in the world is forgiveness. Let go of anger over what happened to you as a child. There is much freedom in forgiving. You can achieve any goal you wish when you let go of blame and move onward and upward in your life. Let go of any tally of wrongs done to you by your parents or other people. Release the past so that you can wake up every morning feeling free and unchained.

Live in the present moment and think positive thoughts about your life. Even in the most difficult of times you can always find something to be grateful about. Strive to live a life of forgiveness and positive thoughts. Release the blame you've put on others and move forward with love in your heart.

I release the past and embrace each moment
with love and forgiveness in my thoughts and heart.

Independence versus Dependency

Emotionally healthy people need people in their lives and desire to be needed by someone. It is a question of balance. Some may not have gotten the love deserved as children, and constantly search for the one who will love them unconditionally. Some are so needy people are driven away. Others become too independent, not allowing themselves to need anyone.

To find balance, the needy can accept the past of not getting the love they deserved. You can parent and love yourself and receive God's love. If the part in you that needs people is closed off, then open up. Take the risk of being vulnerable. Allow yourself to be loved.

I strive for balance in my life by finding peace
in my own company as well as in the presence of others.

Happiness

Happiness comes from within not from outside ourselves. We can be happy by thinking happy thoughts. We are about as happy as we make up our minds to be. It is not easy to do this all the time. It takes practice, strength, courage, and persistence. In any situation in life, if you look hard enough, there is something positive.

Make it a habit to always look for the good. Happiness is strongly connected to attitude. A positive attitude is essential for happiness. Happiness is not always having what you want but wanting what you have.

I look for the good in everything and choose happy, positive thoughts about myself and life.

Mistakes

The best lessons in life are taught by making mistakes. Mistakes help you to grow in character and spirituality.

The most successful people in the world have made the most mistakes. Every mistake contains a lesson to learn. You can only learn from mistakes if you admit them, take responsibility, own them, and then choose differently.

I welcome mistakes in my life as an opportunity
to learn more about myself and to grow spiritually.

Laughter in the Morning

A healthy degree of emotional detachment and hearty laughter every day can stimulate the immune system. Don't take yourself or life too seriously. Laughter is the lubricant of life. It enables you to experience the fullness and joys of life.

Being able to laugh at yourself and the incongruities of everyday situations is the best way to quell stress and to enjoy life. Try this experiment. Every morning for the next week, when you wake up, let the very first thing you do before anything else—before thinking about your day, before going to the bathroom, even before getting out of bed—is to laugh for at least thirty seconds. It's truly a wonderful and positive way to start your day. Laughing first thing in the morning, for no reason at all except to laugh, will make you feel great. Commit to doing it for seven days in a row and see for yourself what a difference it will make. If you live with other people, encourage them to do the same thing.

I choose to see the positive
in everyone and everything around me.

Imagine and Be

To bring anything into your life, your must first imagine that it's already there. If you want more joy, be joyful. If you want more peace, be peaceful. If you want more health, be healthy with every part of your being. Eat healthy foods, exercise, think healthy, positive thoughts, visualize being healthy, breathe health and let go of all negativity such as doubt, worry, and fear.

We are human beings, not human "doings." Above all, remember that you are a co-creator with God. With that type of partnership, anything and everything is possible.

*Creative ideas are revealing themselves
to me each and everyday.*

The Power of Touch

When you are touched in a loving way by another person, your body responds positively. Two hundred hospital patients were studied to test their response to being touched. Half of the patients were to be touched by every staff member who walked into the room, including doctors, nurses, aides, and even the dietitian. The doctor might touch the patient's arm as he asked how the patient was feeling, or a nurse might stroke the patient's hair or shoulder as she gave the medication, and so forth. The other half of the patients were not to be touched at all, except as necessary to perform routine tasks.

Amazingly, the patients who were touched healed three times as fast as the ones who weren't touched. As a result of that study, courses called "The Healing Touch" are now offered to nurses.

You make a connection when you touch another person.

I am optimistic, confident, and self-assured
and I feel good about being close to others.

Thoughts and Expectations

What are your thoughts about wellness? Do you think only healthy thoughts? The body moves along the path of its expectations. There was an interesting experiment conducted with people about to have surgery. They were divided into two groups. The first group dreaded surgery and did everything they could to avoid it. The second group, who had the same medical problems, regarded surgery as a blessing and a chance to free themselves of their illnesses. They thought it was wonderful that science was able to correct their problem so they could be healthy again.

When the surgery was over, it was discovered that those who were confident and looked forward to the surgery had a much better postoperative experience.

God's love heals me and makes me whole.

Loving Yourself

Remember to love yourself. If you want to experience peace and joy, honor your inner higher self and to treat it with respect, kindness, and dignity.

Love yourself. It's only two words to remember. Put signs up all over your home. It is important to remember this every day, every hour. Life has little meaning and will be fraught with difficulty unless you remember to love yourself. When you change your attitude about yourself, everything else changes as well.

The only relationship you ever need to work on is that relationship with yourself. Our lives are a reflection of our predominant feelings toward ourselves. Try this experiment. For the next twenty-four hours, embrace only the most loving, respectful, and positive attitude about yourself. Your life will change for the better.

*The divine breath of God flows through me
and blesses me; all parts of my life fall into place.*

Purifying Your Body

When bogged down by life's stresses, it's time to take extra care of your body—physically, mentally, and spiritually. Here are some things you can do to help rejuvenate and purify your body.

Take a short fast.

Eat just fresh fruits for one or two days.

Go on a short three-day juice fast.

Eat raw foods for seven to ten days.

Get out in the fresh air and exercise.

Meditate and spend some time in solitude.

Take a long, relaxing bath. Put in some relaxing lavender oil.

Give yourself a facial; put on a cleansing mask.

Drink lots of fresh, pure water (not with your meals).

The inner child needs to be nurtured as you purify so that the hurts that caused the imbalance can be understood and released with compassion.

Take *KYO-GREEN* (see *Resources*) daily—a combination of young barley and wheat grass, chlorella cells, brown rice, and kelp. It's an excellent way to rejuvenate and purify your body.

Health is a top priority to me and I take time daily to do all the things that keep me radiantly healthy.

Eat Breakfast

Starting the day with a sensible meal is one of seven factors associated with longevity. A study by UCLA's School of Public Health focused on eating breakfast, never smoking, regular physical activity, moderate or no use of alcohol, seven to eight hours of sleep nightly, maintaining proper weight and not eating between meals. Women who followed all seven could expect to live an average of eight years longer than women who followed only zero to three practices.

A favorite breakfast is fresh fruit in season. When you eat a high fat or high sugar meal early in the morning you might be hungrier during the day and not have as much energy. There's nothing as delicious as fresh fruit in season.

Each morning I give thanks for the gift of life
and the beauty all around me.

Burning More Calories

Every day, you burn calories just by sitting around. Even when you're at rest, your body uses energy to maintain its vital functions.

The amount of energy used at rest varies from person to person and is affected by factors such as age and fat free mass (everything in your body other than fat weight). A 140-pound woman in her thirties will go from burning about 1,510 calories a day at rest to 1,450 by the time she reaches her fifties. Although sixty calories may seem inconsequential, they can translate into a yearly weight gain of about six pounds of fat.

You can raise your metabolism and offset such caloric statistics with exercise. During sustained aerobic exercise your metabolism can rise more than ten times above its resting rate. Additionally, it may remain high for a period of time after exercise.

To promote a long term change in metabolism, you must increase fat free mass, which is mostly muscle. Regular strength training and aerobic exercise will help you build more of this calorie-hungry tissue.

All systems in my body
are expressing high-level wellness and vitality.

Taking Green Magma

Young barley grass offers nature's most complete balance of vitamins, mineral, protein, enzymes, and chlorophyll. Scientist and inventor Yoshihide Hagiwara, MD developed a way to cultivate and process organically grown barley, taking the utmost care in transferring live essential nutrients (from field to package in just three hours) to an easy-to-use, convenient powder form, that is easily and quickly assimilated by our system. This award-winning product is called Green Magma and is available in health food stores (see *Resources*). Mixed with cool water, it's a drink that's excellent for seniors, athletes, children, vegetarians, pregnant women as well as anyone who values optimum health and vitality. I drink it every day.

Green Magma is also available in a Women's Formula with a perfect blend of extra calcium, folic acid and the powerful extracts of six specially-selected "female" Chinese herbs including dong quai and peony root. This natural combination has been used by medical practitioners and herbalists for thousands of years as PMS support and to improve female function. Their unique Green Magma Senior Formula combines the young barley grass with the herbs ginkgo biloba, cat's claw, reishi mushroom, and licorice root. It's even available for dogs and cats under the name of Barley Dog and Barley Cat. I highly recommend all these products.

Health is my natural way of being.

Exercise Your Body, Not Your Face

Your muscles attach to bones almost everywhere on your body, from your neck to your toes. But some of the muscles of the face attach directly to the skin via sinewy fascia attachment. Therefore facial movement actually pulls skin, which promotes wrinkles. That holds true for the chin line as well. Exercises meant to firm the neck and chin can exaggerate the prominence of the platysma muscle, the two vertical bands that run from chin to neck.

The fascia work more efficiently when the body is conditioned because good overall muscle tone helps tighten and firm these elastic connectors, keeping skin taut.

Everyone I see gets a very big smile from me.

Taking Care of Your Teeth

Taking care of your teeth is the best and least-known way to maintain a sharp chin line. Bones, like muscles, stay strong and fit by working against resistance; for the jawbone, teeth are the weights and chewing is the workout. Loose or missing teeth can cause the jaw to shrink and recede, and even a slight shift has an aging effect. Your best protection is to eat a diet high in fresh raw fruits and vegetables that you have to crunch on. The other best prevention is to brush your teeth two or three times a day, floss daily, get regular check-ups and cleaning, and seek immediate treatment for gum flare-ups.

Every time I look in the mirror,
I smile at the beautiful reflection I see.

Plant Foods

Always choose produce that has been organically grown. If you can't determine whether or not the produce has been grown without pesticides, be sure to wash it well before cooking it or eating it raw.

Eat produce in season and that has been grown locally. Many cities have farmers' markets established on special days; they are the best places to buy freshly picked, organically grown produce.

Foods rich in nutrients are an essential part of my wellness lifestyle.

Healthier Baking

Substitute apple sauce for butter or margarine to reduce fat, calories, and cholesterol. Apple sauce provides moisture and stability when used as a fat alternative, performing best in recipes containing other moist ingredients such as skim milk or fresh fruit.

You can make fresh apple sauce simply by putting cut up apples, peeled or unpeeled, depending on your preference, in your blender. For chunkier apple sauce, blend for a few seconds. For smoother sauce, blend for a minute or more. For variety, sprinkle in some cinnamon while blending and stir in some raisins after blended.

Everyday I am healthier and younger.

Fruit for Fiber

Fruit is more than just great tasting food. It's also a superb source of fiber, with most varieties supplying from ten to twenty-five percent of your daily needs per serving. This is good news not just for your intestines, as the insoluble fiber can help reduce the risk of colon cancer, but also for your arteries, because fresh fruit supplies ample amount of cholesterol-lowering soluble fiber as well.

The fiber-rich guava helps lower moderately elevated cholesterol levels by ten percent. The fiber in fruit also appears to have a talent for prolonging feelings of satiation after eating, possibly by slowing digestion within the stomach. The high sugar content of fruit is not detrimental to your health. Fruit sugar is slowly released into the blood because of the fiber and the sugar's form being fructose. If you're concerned about controlling your weight, consider a diet rich in fruit.

I appreciate my body temple and keep it healthy
by eating several pieces of fruit every day.

Skating

Rollerblading (known as in-line skating) is fast becoming one of the hottest workouts. You really feel it in your legs, buttocks, and hips, because you have to push off each time. It's an excellent lower body activity.

Most people learn in smooth, traffic-free areas like bike trails or company parking lots on weekends. The first thing you have to learn is how to stop. Lifting up your toe will drive the brake into the ground, and you'll skid to an eventual halt. Other advice for beginners: avoid downhill slopes and traffic, and don't wear headphones, which can prevent you from hearing what is coming at or behind you.

Skating is also a great way to keep your inner child alive. Feeling the breeze on your face and hair and gliding gently as you push is a wonderful, freeing feeling. It's a great way to add variety into your aerobic workouts.

I skate through life with love in my heart
and a smile on my face.

What about Polyunsaturated Fat?

Margarine, corn oil, and other sources of poly-unsaturated fat have long been touted as safe alternatives to saturated fats. In fact, they are far less healthful than once thought and may be more harmful than saturated. Perhaps the worst fat of all is partially hydrogenated vegetable oil.

Polyunsaturated fat not only raises levels of LDL (bad) cholesterol, but also reduces levels of HDL (good) cholesterol. And polyunsaturated fat may promote the growth of cancer cells.

Cancer rates in the United States began to rise just about the time polyunsaturated fats began to replace saturated fats in the American diet. To be safe, limit your intake of all fats, saturated and polyunsaturated fat in particular.

I love my body and honor it
by feeding it only healthy foods.

Working Out

Exercise increases creativity. A new study examined 120 people and divided them into two groups—one that ran twenty minutes twice a week for eight weeks and one that did no exercise at all. Tested on their creativity both before and after the program, participants in the nonexercise group showed no change, while the runners improved exceptionally. It was found that when you do aerobic exercise, you go into a brain wave shift from left brain logical thinking into a right brain, nonlinear, creative state. Even after one session, creativity improved.

I enjoy making my body healthy and happy
by exercising regularly.

Anti-Aging Nutrients

Vitamin C: Antioxidant. Helps protect against free-radical damage caused by pollutants, and helps block formation of cancer-causing substances like nitrosamines. May reduce risk of cancer of mouth, esophagus, and stomach. May lower risk of cataracts, may slow or prevent decline in immunity, and interfere with damaging effects of LDL cholesterol.

Vitamin D: Helps absorb and metabolize calcium to keep bones healthy and strong.

Vitamin E: Antioxidant. May protect against pancreatic and oral cancers, and heart disease, improve immunity, and lower risk of cataracts. Protective against environmental toxins that contribute to emphysema-like diseases.

Calcium: Helps prevent osteoporosis. May reduce risk of colon cancer.

Selenium: Antioxidant. May reduce incidence of some cancers, ward off infection and possibly protect against heart disease.

Beta-carotene: Antioxidant. May reduce the risk of lung, breast, colon, prostate, and cervical cancer. May slow or prevent the age-related decline in immunity. May block the damage LDL (bad) cholesterol does to arteries.

*I protect my body against disease
by eating a wide variety of fresh fruits and vegetables,
whole grains, legumes, nuts, and seeds.*

Some Healthy Food Tips

Replace coffee with herbal tea that doesn't contain caffeine. Evidence suggests that oregano, rosemary, lemon balm, sage, spearmint, savory, thyme, and peppermint all contain significant levels of antioxidants. To conserve the vitamin E in your herbs, bring your tea water to a boil, then turn off the heat and drop in the herb or just pour boiling water over the herb.

Use plenty of wild greens, such as purslane, in a daily salad. This wonder weed has two to ten times as much vitamin E as spinach. Of course, use tame leaves like spinach and chicory, too. Usually the greener the leaf, the more antioxidants. For dressing, try citrus juice and a small amount of extra virgin cold pressed olive oil.

Eat one or two Brazil nuts a day to help save yourself and the rain forest. The average Brazil nut contains more than your RDA in the antioxidant selenium.

Eat a handful of raw sunflower seeds every day—not to exceed one ounce. Sunflower seeds are one of the better sources of vitamin E.

*I nourish my body with natural foods
as close to the way God made them.*

Another Reason
to Eat Your Vegetables

Women who consume lots of fruits and vegetables and who also supplement their diets with
vitamin C help reduce their risk for all cancers.

As women increase their intake of vegetables and
fruits, fruits alone and dietary vitamin C, their risk for
all cancers and for colon cancer decreases. Women who
take a vitamin A or vitamin C supplement are also less
likely to develop colon cancer. As the intake of these
nutrients increases, women's lung cancer risk decreases.

*I breathe in health and vitality
and exhale all tensions and worries.*

Eat More and Weigh Less

Eat any of the following until you are full: legumes, fruits, whole grains, and vegetables.

Emphasize complex carbohydrates. Add flavor without adding fat; dress up your carbohydrates with herbs and spices. Complex carbohydrates are low in calories, high in fiber and bulky, so they fill you up before you eat too much. Simple carbohydrates—table sugar, alcohol, honey, molasses, corn syrup—do not fill you up. They have no fiber and are not at all bulky.

Eat in moderation, depending on fat content: nonfat or low fat products such as egg whites, nonfat yogurts and cheeses, fat free crackers, nonfat mayonnaise or sour cream, low fat frozen dinners.

Avoid meat. If you must eat meat, try small amounts of roasted or grilled skinless chicken breast or fish. Even fish and chicken contain essentially no fiber and no complex carbohydrates.

Forego oils. This includes most salad dressings and especially margarine because they are simply liquid or pure fat.

Being overweight is directly related to how much fat you consume, most of which comes from animal products and oils. But if you follow these guidelines, you can lose weight and keep it off.

*My food choices reflect my strong commitment
to being healthy and living fully.*

KYOLIC

Studies by Dr. Robert I-San Lin and Dr. Manfred Steiner found that *KYOLIC* Aged Garlic Extract (see *Resources*) and its active compounds are potent inhibitors of platelet adhesion; the only other substance known to have this property of tocopherol, a form of vitamin E. This major breakthrough in the search for prevention of cardiovascular disease is consistent with prior discoveries of the protective effects of garlic.

KYOLIC's active compounds inhibit the growth and multiplication of the lining cells that have been induced to grow and to form an arteriosclerotic mass. This discovery is not only a major advance in arteriosclerotic research, but has an important implication on cancer prevention, too. The abnormal growth of arteriosclerotic tissue share some characteristics of cancer, and *KYOLIC* also inhibits cancer cell growth and multiplication.

In another study, Dr. Lin found that *KYOLIC* minimized carcinogen-induced mammary (breast) cancer development and inhibited the growth of cultured human cancer cells.

*My entire body is a radiant expression
of health and vitality.*

Pregnancy and Jogging

Should you continue to workout if you're pregnant? Slow down, but don't stop. A Pennsylvania State University study compared two groups of pregnant women, runners and sedentary women. The runners pretty much continued their usual regimens, but instinctively cut back thirty-three to fifty percent the last trimester. The sedentary women also continued their usual regimens.

The running moms gained less weight and had slightly smaller babies (averaging about a half pound less), but the lower weight wasn't enough to put the babies at risk. And it made delivery easier on their moms.

Check with your physician about activity during pregnancy, and don't try to maintain your prepregnancy regimen for the whole nine months.

*My body is filled with the life force of God
and I celebrate living fully.*

Protect Your Hearing

Live rock music ranks right up there with thunder and stereo headphones at full volume as posing an immediate danger of hearing loss. Even worse are the sounds of a gunshot or a jet plane takeoff, capable of causing actual pain and eventual hearing loss.

A good rule to protect your sense of hearing: if you have to shout to be heard over the noise, you need hearing protection. Next time you go to a concert, or a night club with music, put in some ear plugs that are soft and comfortable in your ears. These also work well if you sleep with someone who snores.

In quiet and solitude,
I listen to the whisperings of my higher self.

Strong Hamstrings

The back of your thigh and your buttocks are easy to firm and tone with this exercise.

Wearing ankle weights, kneel and place your forearms on the ground, slightly ahead of your shoulders, keeping your spine and neck in straight line. With your abdomen pulled in and weight transferred to your left forearm, raise your straightened right leg so your knee is in line with buttocks and your foot is flexed. Curl your heel in to your buttocks as far as is comfortable; hold. Slowly extend your leg back and out to a straightened position. Repeat sets on your left side.

An easier version: Lie face down on the floor, arms under your hips, right leg lifted slightly. Flex your toe, curl your heel into your buttocks, hold, then straighten.

The easiest version: If the previous one strains your back, curl your heel from the floor rather than from suspended position; use lighter weights if needed.

My legs and buttocks are toned and shapely and all my clothes fit me perfectly.

Cookware

You can buy the best quality foods with the highest nutritional value but if you cook them improperly, you'll lose lots of nutrients. Stainless steel cookware is unsurpassed for the best in cooking for optimum health. Fresh foods can be cooked without additional water, oil, fat, butter, or margarine. The brand I use and recommend is Neova.

The waterless and greaseless Neova cookware can revitalize your cooking by creating healthier foods with more robust flavor. Not only will your meals taste better, but Neova cookware will calm the dinner hour routine by doing half of the work for you. You can trust this stainless steel cookware not to release aluminum, rust, porcelain chips or Teflon flakes into your food. And you will be caring more for the environment's future by using Neova cookware, because it will last to the next generation.

If you would like more information about the Neova cookware and its accompanying 121-page cookbook, see *Resources*.

I take pleasure in selecting and preparing foods
in a healthy way. I give thanks for all my meals.

Super Healing Fruits

Pears: This high water content fruit is a great source of fiber. In addition to all its other benefits, fiber (when combined with a low fat diet) can lessen the risk of developing polyps in the colon, which may be a precursor to cancer. Pears also provide some vitamin C, potassium, and boron.

Strawberries: There's more vitamin C and fiber in strawberries than you'll find in most fruits, including oranges. (In fact, any berry is an excellent source of fiber.) Strawberries also contain ellagic acid, a natural cancer-fighting chemical. Researchers have found that this compound is a potent inhibitor of such carcinogens as tobacco smoke and nitrosamines. Ellagic acid is even more concentrated in strawberry juice, especially when combined with pineapple juice.

Prunes: The high fiber content of prunes makes them a classic source of relief for constipation. They are also a bone-saving source of boron and of the antioxidant vitamins A and E. Some prunes each day will definitely keep constipation away.

*I am grateful for my digestive system
which is healthy and happy.*

Snacks for Kids

Growing children should be encouraged to snack. Snacking provides twenty-five to thirty percent of a child's daily required caloric intake.

While parents enjoy sitting down to more substantial meals, their children may prefer to snack. Adult portions may be overwhelming to children and snack portions are small and better suited to a child's appetite.

Healthy snacks are the preferred choice. Children who have not been inundated with junk food tend to be fairly healthy eaters. Parents should encourage their offspring to eat natural, low fat snacks. Fresh fruits, raw vegetables, popcorn, fruit bars, and freshly made juices are all good choices. Keep a good supply on hand and they will get eaten.

It also helps if parents set a good example. It will be difficult to persuade your child to eat carrot or celery sticks if you sit down to a hot fudge sundae.

I give my inner child permission to come out and play and celebrate this wonderful day.

Rest and Exercise

It's best to rest one or two days each week in-between bouts of exercise for a balanced training program. The body must have time to replenish the glycogen (blood sugar) lost during training. Weak muscles drained of energy are more prone to injuries. If trained hard without resting, the body cannot regenerate the muscle filaments, which can cause damage in the long term.

You can rest guilt free each week from exercise. Take your rest days and do some longer stretching, yoga, and take a gentle walk in nature.

I take time out each day for some self nurturing and let solitude be an important ingredient to living fully.

We Are What We Eat

Hardly a month goes by without publication of another major study showing the importance of eating fruits and vegetables to prevent disease. Here are some recent studies.

A survey of female nurses by Harvard Medical School found that women who eat lots of fruit and vegetables cut their risk of stroke by fifty-four percent. Spinach and carrots, with the antioxidant vitamins (beta-carotene, C and E), were quite effective.

In a related study of males at the University of Texas, men whose diet contained amounts of vitamin C and beta-carotene obtained from one to two oranges and carrots per day had a thirty percent lower risk of dying from heart disease.

Another study of male health professionals by Harvard School of Public Health found that men with the highest intake of potassium, contained in fruits and vegetables, reduced their risk of kidney stones by half.

Everyday I eat a variety of fruits and vegetables
to keep my marvelous body temple in radiant health.

Skin Care

To soothe dry skin, add a cup of milk to your bath water. The protein softens and moisturizes your skin. Make sure to apply a moisturizer after the bath while the skin is still damp.

Take bath time to also soothe your mind. Let go of tensions and negative thoughts. Light a few candles and listen to some relaxing music. When your body is calm and relaxed, it is reflected on your face. Make this a time of turning within, listening to your inner guidance and finding the peace of your own company.

Each week take some extra time to pamper yourself.

My body is a safe and pleasurable place to be.

Figuring Your Target Heart Rate

By keeping track of your heart rate, you can evaluate whether your are working out as hard as you need to in order to get your heart in top shape. To find your target heart rate, take your age and subtract it from 220 to get your maximal heart rate, then multiply that number by 0.7. The result is your target heart rate, seventy percent of your maximal rate. Once you have figured that out, you know about how many times per minute your heart should beat when you're exercising. So when you're riding a stationary bike, take your pulse rate for ten seconds, then multiply that number by six to get the number of beats per minute. Always remember that the better your level of conditioning, the harder it will be to reach your target rate.

Don't worry if your have some trouble monitoring your heart rate at the start; it will become easier with practice and monitoring your heart rate won't cut into the quality of your training if you stop pedaling for ten seconds to check it. On a lot of the stationary bikes coming out now, there are different types of easy to use pulse monitors. You can also get pulse monitors for other sports, like jogging.

Today I give myself the gift of exercise
to honor my body temple.

Healthy Tips

Vegetarians are on average thinner than non-vegetarians, despite greater caloric intake, and have a greater sex drive. Eating more vegetables and less meat increases one's energy and vitality.

Here are some more interesting facts. Lonely people have higher levels of cholesterol; developing a sense of intimacy can enhance our health, our well-being, even our survival. Individuals with good social support systems tend to have lower blood cholesterol levels and better immune functions, independent of other factors.

Eating a vegetable-rich diet doesn't necessarily raise your intake of pesticide residues. The pesticide content of fruits and vegetables is well below that of meat, which comes from animals raised on pesticide-sprayed crops. To minimize your intake of potential toxins, buy organic produce.

I enjoy making a variety of fruits and vegetables an essential part of my healthy diet.

Keep Yourself Fit

Mind and body are one; train physically as well as mentally to reach your full potential. Exercise is a key element for self-mastery and living fully. Not only does exercise promote optimum health, but also mental clarity, greater physical and mental strength, and a more youthful appearance. Exercise tones and defines the body, makes you feel more confident, increases your endurance, helps you to lose or maintain weight, and also has been found to reduce stress in the body.

A single dose of exercise works better than tranquilizers (and without undesirable side effects) as a muscle relaxant for people with symptoms of anxiety tension. Movement is strong medicine.

*I am relaxed in body, mind, and spirit
and love in the presence of love.*

Getting the Most from Fruit

To reap the most benefit from eating fruit, eat a well-selected mix of fruit every day. Eat one serving a day of a type rich in vitamin C and another serving rich in beta-carotene for fruit's antioxidant powers. Add to that varieties rich in fiber and potassium for the good of your bowels, cholesterol levels, and blood pressure.

Shop for fruit that's in season for the best selection and peak nutrient content. Select firm, plump fruit with good color and no bruises or breaks in the skin. Avoid oversized pieces of fruit since they are often not as sweet as smaller pieces. Fruit that is hard and not yet ripe also should be avoided as it probably won't ripen to your satisfaction at home. Store ripe fruit in the refrigerator, and eat within a few days if possible. When preparing fruit, rinse in cool water but avoid soaking since some fruits can become waterlogged to the point of losing nutrient content. If slicing fruit, eat as soon as possible in order to take advantage of peak nutrient content.

Fruit provides me with an abundance of energy.

Living with Reverence

There is a higher power within you that's available to guide you every moment of your life. Some choose to call it God, the essence of being. You cannot know this intellectually, you cannot substantiate it, nor can you debate it. You can simply feel it and become aware of it.

When you become aware of it, joy permeates your being and you begin to live with a perpetual feeling of reverence. Our Creator, the very self of each one of us, never would have made us had He not loved us. Allow this thought to fill your heart with devotion and gratitude. Look around and remind yourself that every instant is filled with God; this will bring you a profound feeling of awe and worship. There are no ordinary moments.

When the feeling of reverence for life is most intense you will be the closest to God and your life will be filled with joy and blessings. These deep feelings of awe are inexpressible; in the act of devotion and adoration, silence is the highest praise.

All is well in my life; I am truly blessed.

A Forty-Eight Hour
Experiment in Love

Love may be experienced in many ways, yet love is one. It is the fountain of God that gives meaning to life and is a source of profound joy and peace. The ancient Greeks made a distinction between erotic love (Eros), brotherly love (Philia), and the love of God (Agape). Whether romantic love, parental love, love of beauty, nature, or love of life, all forms reflect the unconditional love associated with healing. The mystery of love can be experienced in many ways and may be called by many names, yet it remains unchanged.

Whenever you choose to pay attention to love, you strengthen your capacity for healing. Always remember that the divine, or God, is in heaven, earth, and inside you. It can be felt by living from love. If you are willing to love as much as you can from wherever you are, your life will be transformed for the better. Experiment for the next two days. Endeavor to have the happiest most joyous, most loving feeling that you can create at every moment. If you do this and nothing more, your entire life will change for the better within forty-eight hours.

Everything I think, feel, and do
is imbued with the feeling of love.

Steps to a Balanced Life

Keep fit. Get plenty of exercise, sleep, water, and nutritious foods.

Learn to relax. Keep your stress level under control. Get involved in sports and recreational activities. Pursue a hobby. Learn deep-relaxation techniques, such as meditation, yoga, and breathing exercises.

Rid yourself of negative emotions. Find a way to clear up your negative feelings as thoroughly and quickly as possible.

Embrace gratitude. No matter what is going on in your life, be grateful. Gratitude can transform your life and create miracles.

Practice forgiveness. Forgive yourself and others on a daily basis. It will heal and enrich the quality of your life.

I choose to see problems as wonderful opportunities.

Steps to Living a Balanced Life II

Visualize your goals and dreams daily. Your thoughts determine your experiences. Think positively about those things you want to become part of your life.

Find time each day to be alone. Enjoy the peace of your own company.

Simplify your life. You have a choice; you are not a victim of your environment. Slow down.

Develop a sense of humor. A healthy degree of emotional detachment and hearty laughter every day can stimulate the immune system. Don't take yourself or life too seriously. Laughter enables you to experience the fullness and joys of life.

Be loving. Nothing will change your life more quickly than embracing a consistent feeling of love in your heart.

A healthy lifestyle is more than eating right and exercising regularly. Make a commitment to yourself to enrich each day from a physical, mental, emotional, and spiritual standpoint. By putting this balance into your life, you'll reap the rewards of getting more out of living—happily, passionately, and healthfully.

*I am committed to living fully—
happily, healthfully, passionately, and peacefully.*

You Are Unique

Spend time today pondering the idea of how absolutely unique, special, and marvelous you truly are. Over this past year, you've thought a lot about your life and what you want and have grown to love and respect who you are. Always remember that there is no one else in the world, either in the past or in the future, who is exactly like you.

You are unique and absolutely special. Celebrate your uniqueness today and choose to live more fully — passionately, healthfully, joyfully, and peacefully — in every area of your life.

I wish you peace and salute your great adventure.
Lovingly,

Susan S. Jones

From this day forward, I choose to continue living fully — passionately, peacefully, and joyfully.

Resources

All One People, Nutritech, 719 Haley Street, Santa Barbara, CA 93103, (800) 235-5727

All One is a pure nutrient powder I have used for years. Delicious when mixed with your favorite juice, All One provides over fifty vitamins, minerals, and amino acids. Call or write for more information and a free sample of All One.

Aloe Falls, Yerba Prima, Inc., 740 Jefferson Avenue, Ashland, OR 97520-3743

Aloe Falls by Yerba Prima is preservative-free, great tasting, and Certified Active, which means that Aloe Falls is laboratory-verified to provide the health benefits of aloe. Their Aloe Juice Formula contains 50 percent aloe vera and a powerful herbal blend of peppermint, chamomile, and parsley to boost its soothing properties in your digestive system. Yerba Prima products are available at your local health food store. Write for more information.

American Natural Hygiene Society, *Health Science* Magazine, James M. Lennon, P.O. Box 30630, Tampa, FL 33630, (813) 855-6607

This wonderful organization publishes the award-winning *Health Science* magazine. Annual membership dues are $25.00 which includes a subscription to *Health Science.* Members also receive discounts on health books, videos, and cassette programs, seminars, lectures, and more. Write and become a member today.

Bionic Products, 466 Central Avenue, Suite 20, North-
field, IL 60093, (847) 441-6000, (800) 634-4667

Bionic Products markets the Elanra Therapeutic Ionizer. Elanra delivers small, ingestable negative ions essential for proper ion balance. Call or write for more
information.

Bio-Strath, Bioforce of America, 122 Smith Road Extension, Kinderhook, NY 12106, (800) 645-7198

Bio-Strath is an excellent liquid herbal food supplement. It has been found to combat fatigue, lethargy,
and nervousness, increase physical and mental efficiency, reinforce the immune defense system and restore
vitality. Available from your local health food stores or
call for ordering information.

BodySlant & Body Lift, P.O. Box 1667, Newport Beach,
CA 92663, (800) 443-3917

This superb slant board also functions as a bed and
ottoman. I recommend using it daily. The Body Lift is
a simple and comfortable way to stand your body upside
down so that your shoulders rest on a thick cushion,
your head dangles off the floor, and your neck stretches
naturally. I use the BodySlant daily and highly recommend it for better health, vitality, and rejuvenation. Call
or write for more information or to order.

CamoCare, Abkit, Inc., 207 East 94th Street, New York,
NY 10128, (800) 226-2273

CamoCare is a marvelous line of natural skincare products based on a special chamomile flower from Europe and is available in health food stores.

Center for Conservative Therapy, 4310 Lichau Road, Penngrove, CA 94951, (707) 792-2325

Founded by Drs. Alan Goldhamer and Jennifer Marano, this center offers an alternative approach to the restoration and maintenance of optimum health. The focus is on helping people make diet and lifestyle changes, and also offers certified supervised fasting.

DeSouza Chlorophyll Products, P.O. Box 395, Dept. SJ, Beaumont, CA 92220, (800) 373-5171

DeSouza's liquid chlorophyll (available in tablets and capsules) and other personal care products are very beneficial for enhancing health. Call or write for more information, a catalog, or to place an order.

EarthSave, 706 Frederick Street, Santa Cruz, CA 95062-2205, (408) 423-4069

Founded by John Robbins, author of *Diet for a New America* and *May All Be Fed,* EarthSave is a nonprofit organization providing educational and leadership for transition to more healthful and environmentally sound food choices, nonpolluting energy supplies, and a wiser use of natural resources. Call or write for their catalog of books, audio and videotapes, and other products.

Ester-C, Inter-Cal Corporation, 533 Madison Avenue, Prescott, AZ 86301, (520) 445-8063

Inter-Cal is the manufacturer of Ester-C calcium ascorbate. Ester-C is formulated in a wide variety of nutritional supplements and can be found on the shelves of health food stores, drug, stores, and supermarkets. If you can't find a source, call or write Inter-Cal.

Fortified Flax, Omega-Life, Inc. P.O. Box 208, Brookfield, WI 53008-0208, (414) 786-2070, (800) 328-3529

Fortified Flax is one of the best sources of Omega-3 fatty acids, along with soluble and insoluble fiber, plus a great source of lignans. This brand is fortified with the proper vitamins and minerals to help the essential fatty acids in flax metabolize properly, as well as keep the ground seed fresh. Call or write for more information.

Green Foods Corporation, 320 N. Graves Avenue, Oxnard, CA 93030, (800) 222-3374, ext. 434

This excellent company offers a top quality line of barley grass juice products. Some of their products include Green Magma, Green Essence, Green Magma Senior Formula, Green Magma Women's Formula, Beta Carrot, Wheat Germ Extract, and Barley Dog. Green barley juice is a perfect balance of vitamins, minerals, enzymes, protein, and chlorophyll. Call or write for more information or to order.

Susan Smith Jones, Ph.D. Workshops, Lectures, Seminars, Keynote Addresses, 3-Day Retreats (800) 345-8255

If you would like to schedule Dr. Jones to give a motivational presentation to your corporation, community, church or school group, call for more information.

Audiocassette tapes by Dr. Susan Smith Jones

Celebrate Life! Seven-cassette series includes fourteen different programs and six guided meditations

    1a. *The Main Ingredients: Positive Thinking and the Mind*

    1b. *The Main Ingredients: Exercise, Nutrition and Relaxation*

    2a. *Get High on Life Through Exercise*

    2b. *Make Your Exercise Program a Great Adventure*

    3a. *Nutrition for Aliveness*

    3b. *Superlative Dining*

    4a. *Your Thoughts May Be Fattening*

    4b. *Living Lightly, Naturally Trim*

    5a. *Experience Aliveness*

    5b. *Learn From Children How To Celebrate Life*

    6a. *The Joy of Solitude and The Art of Serenity*

    6b. *Relaxation and Meditation: Natural and Easy*

    7a. *Celebrate Your Magnificence*

    7b. *Affirm a Beautiful Life*

To order the entire seven-tape album, send $80.00 or $15.00 per tape (US check or money order only), payable to: Health Unlimited, P.O. Box 49396, Los Angeles, CA 90049. For more information on the tapes, send a business size, stamped, self-addressed envelope to the above address. For credit card orders, call (800) 843-5743 (PST).

Learn To Live A Balanced Life
A Fresh Start: Rejuvenate Your Body
Making Your Life a Great Adventure

These three 2-tape programs above were recorded live from Susan's popular motivational workshops. Together all three make a complete program designed to show you how to live an empowered, balanced life and how to tie the physical, mental, emotional, and spiritual aspects of life together to create a holistic approach to successful living.

Price: $25.00 each or all three for $60.00. Make checks (US check or money order only) payable to: Health Unlimited, P.O. Box 49396, Los Angeles, CA 90049 or call (800) 843-5743 (PST). Ask about Susan's books on tape, too.

How To Achieve Any Goal: The Magic of Creative Visu-alization—Living Your Vision/Commitment

A one and a half hour audiocassette by Susan Smith Jones. Includes a twenty-minute meditation you can use every day to help you realize your goals and dreams. To order, please send $15.00 (US check or money order only) payable to: Health Unlimited, P.O. Box 49396, Los Angeles, CA 90049.

Kyo-Green, Kyolic Aged Garlic Extract, and Gingko Biloba Plus, Wakunaga of America Co., Ltd., 23501 Madero, Mission Viejo, CA 92691, (800) 825-7888

These are all excellent nutritional supplements available at your local health food store. Call or write for more information or free samples of these products.

Mori-Nu Silken "Lite" Tofu, Morinaga, 2050 West 190th Street, Suite 110, Torrance, CA 90504

This is a very healthy source of low fat protein. For more information and delicious recipes, send a self-addressed stamped envelope.

Mountain Valley Growers, 38325 Pepperweed Road, Squaw Valley, CA 93675, (209) 338-2775

Since its inception in 1983, Mountain Valley Growers has been testing new herb varieties so only the most flavorful and prolific plants will make it to the customer. Over 400 varieties of organically grown plants can be shipped anywhere in the US. Call or write for more information and a catalog.

Peace Pilgrim, Friends of Peace Pilgrim, 43480 Cedar Avenue, Hemet, CA 92544, (909) 927-7678

To receive a free thirty-two page booklet, *Steps Toward Inner Peace,* a free 216-page book, *Peace Pilgrim,* a free video documentary or an inspiring newsletter, write to the above address. Friends of Peace Pilgrim is a non-profit, tax-exempt, all-volunteer organization.

PowerBar, PowerFood, Inc., 2448 6th Street, Berkeley, CA 94710, (800) 444-5154

The PowerBar is a delicious, sustained energy bar for endurance, used by athletes and active people. It's also low in fat. Available in health food and fitness stores and some super markets.

Premier One Products, Inc., 1500 Kearns Boulevard, Park City, UT 84060, (800) 373-9660

Premier One swarms like a beehive with energetic people who believe in their products. They pride themselves with providing products in their raw, whole state. They have recently introduced a number of combination products-including Raw Energy and BeeVive-for energy and rejuvenation. Call or write for more information and a catalog.

Self-Realization Fellowship, 3880 San Rafael Avenue, Los Angeles, CA 90065, (213) 225-2471

Write for more information on Paramahansa Yogananda, his books, meditation, home study lessons, the locations of the Self-Realization Fellowship centers, or a catalog of their books, tapes, quarterly magazine, and other products.

Soft Heat Sauna, 4828 Pacific Road NE, Calgary, Alberta T2S 5S5, Canada, (800) 763-4328

Taking saunas has been an important part of my health program for more than twenty years. Soft Heat Sauna makes a top quality, unique sauna for home or office. It's excellent for weight control, skin cleansing, pain relief, stress reduction, stiff joints, and cardiovascular fitness. Call or write for more information.

Spectrum Naturals, Inc., 133 Copeland Street, Petaluma, CA 94952, (800) 995-2705

Producers of Veg Omega-3 Organic Flax Seed Oil, Spectrum Spread, Wheat Germ Oil, natural vegetable oils, pure pressed without chemicals, and a variety of natural, delicious condiments. Call or write for more information and their consumer education series on healthy oils.

Trace-Lyte, Nature's Path, Inc., P.O. Box 7862, Venice, FL 34287 (800) 326-5772, Fax (941) 426-6871

Nature's Path manufactures a top quality crystalloid electrolyte formula, Trace-Lyte, which I take and recommend. This liquid promotes homeostasis in the body. Nature's Path manufactures a number of other quality products that synergistically combine with electrolytes. Call or write for more information.

Vita-Mix Total Nutrition Center and Neova, Vita-Mix Corporation, 8615 Usher Road, Cleveland, OH 44138, (800) 848-2649

Substituting health-building, whole food nutrition in place of devitalized, packaged food is fast and convenient with the Vita-Mix Total Nutrition Center. Turn fruits and vegetables into "whole food" juices in less than four minutes. Freeze a 1/2 gallon of all-fruit ice cream in less than 60 seconds. Grind whole wheat into flour for bread or pancake batter in seconds. The machine performs 35 processes in all. Neova is a top quality, stainless steel cookware that I use and highly recommend. Mention *Choose to Live Each Day Fully* when you call or write for further information or to order.

Westbrae Natural/Westsoy, 1065 E. Walnut Avenue, Carson, CA 90746, (310) 886-8200, (800) 769-6455

Westbrae makes a complete line of non-dairy, organic milk alternatives in addition to a variety of healthy food items (soups, beans, snacks) available in natural food stores. Call or write for more information on their products, samples, and product coupons.

If this book has moved you into action and enriched your life, do yourself and others a favor by giving copies as gifts. As you give, you receive. Remember, we're all here on this earth not to see through one another, but to see one another through and assist others on their journey. Share this book with your relatives and friends. Those wishing to have their own copies may obtain them by calling: (800) 843-5743 (PST).

Index to Days

About the Author

Susan Smith Jones is a leading voice for health, fitness and peaceful living in America today. She not only teaches wellness, she lives it. In 1985, Susan was selected as one of ten Healthy American Fitness Leaders by The President's Council on Physical Fitness and Sports, and in 1988, the President's Council designated Susan as National Master in weight training.

Susan's credentials include a doctorate in health sciences, a master's degree in kinesiology and a bachelor's in psychology. She has been a fitness instructor to students, staff, and faculty at UCLA for over 20 years. But she is probably best known as an advocate of healthy, peaceful living and positive thinking. She is the author of ten books, appears regularly on radio and television talk shows, and has written more than 500 magazine articles.

Susan also travels internationally as a health and fitness consultant and motivational speaker for community, corporate, and church groups. Her inspiring keynote presentations and workshops are often scheduled one to two years in advance. As a health and fitness trainer, she develops personalized wellness programs for individuals and families.

Susan is founder and president of Health Unlimited, a Los Angeles-based consulting firm dedicated to the advancement of human potential, health education, and peaceful living. She has acquired the nickname of "Sunny" and lives in Brentwood, Los Angeles.

Other Celestial Arts books you may enjoy

Choose to be Healthy
by Susan Smith Jones, Ph.D.
The choices we make in life can greatly increase our health and happiness — this book details how to analyze one's choices about food, exercise, thought, work and play, and then use this information to create a better, healthier life. 264 pages

Choose to Live Peacefully
by Susan Smith Jones, Ph.D.
By nurturing our inner selves and living in personal peace, we can help to bring about global change. In this book, Susan Smith-Jones explores the many components of a peaceful, satisfying life — including exercise, nutrition, solitude, meditation, ritual, and environmental awareness — and shows how they can be linked to world peace. 310 pages

Staying Healthy with Nutrition
by Elson Haas, M.D.
The long-awaited examination of how what we eat determines our health and well-being. Truly a complete reference work, it details every aspect of nutrition from drinking water to medicinal foods to the latest biochemical research. 1,200 pages

Staying Healthy with the Seasons
by Elson Haas, M.D.
One of the most popular of the new health books, this is a blend of Eastern and Western medicines, nutrition, herbology, exercise, and preventive healthcare. 260 pages

Ship to:

Name _____

Address _____

City _____ State _____ Zip _____

Phone _____

For Visa and MasterCard orders call (800) 841-BOOK.
CELESTIAL ARTS • P.O. Box 7123, Berkeley, CA 94707